TRADING REALITIES

THE TRUTH, THE LIES, AND THE HYPE IN-BETWEEN

JEFF AUGEN

Vice President, Publisher: Tim Moore
Associate Publisher and Director of Marketing: Amy Neidlinger
Executive Editor: Jim Boyd
Editorial Assistant: Pamela Boland
Development Editor: Russ Hall
Operations Manager: Gina Kanouse
Senior Marketing Manager: Julie Phifer
Publicity Manager: Laura Czaja
Assistant Marketing Manager: Megan Colvin
Cover Designer: Chuti Prasertsith
Managing Editor: Kristy Hart
Project Editor: Betsy Harris
Copy Editors: Apostrophe Editing Services and Krista Hansing Editorial Services, Inc.
Proofreader: Kathy Ruiz
Indexer: Joy Dean Lee
Compositor: TnT Design
Manufacturing Buyer: Dan Uhrig

Publishing as FT Press
Upper Saddle River, New Jersey 07458

Printed in the United States of America

First Printing October 2010

ISBN-10: 0-13-707009-8
ISBN-13: 978-0-13-707009-1

Pearson Education LTD.
Pearson Education Australia PTY, Limited.
Pearson Education Singapore, Pte. Ltd.
Pearson Education Asia, Ltd.
Pearson Education Canada, Ltd.
Pearson Educatión de Mexico, S.A. de C.V.
Pearson Education—Japan
Pearson Education Malaysia, Pte. Ltd.

Library of Congress Cataloging-in-Publication Data

Augen, Jeffrey
Trading realities : the truth, the lies, and the hype in- between / Jeff Augen.
p. cm.
ISBN 978-0-13-707009-1 (hbk. : alk. paper)
1. Investments. 2. Speculation. 3. Capital market. I. Title.
HG4521.A87155 2011
332.6—dc22

2010032969

To Takahashi Sensei who represents the very best of everything—focus, discipline, hard work, and unending dedication to achieving perfection.

Contents

Acknowledgments

I'd like to thank the team that helped pull the book together. Most important was Betsy Harris whose patience and flexibility compensated for the fact that I missed every deadline. Writing books takes time, but publishing them takes professional-level attention to detail. As always, I put the words on the paper but Betsy turned them into a book.

The other requirement for success is a publisher who is willing to explore new concepts. Jim Boyd fills that role by encouraging new ideas. As a result, the final manuscript ended up being much different than what I originally envisioned. Jim always steers me in the right direction.

About the Author

Jeff Augen, currently a private investor and writer, has spent more than a decade building a unique intellectual property portfolio of databases, algorithms, and associated software for technical analysis of derivatives prices. His work, which includes more than a million lines of computer code, is particularly focused on the identification of subtle anomalies and price distortions.

Augen has a 25-year history in information technology. As cofounding executive of IBM's Life Sciences Computing business, he defined a growth strategy that resulted in $1.2 billion of new revenue and managed a large portfolio of venture capital investments. From 2002 to 2005, Augen was President and CEO of TurboWorx Inc., a technical computing software company founded by the chairman of the Department of Computer Science at Yale University. His books include *Day Trading Options*, *Trading Options at Expiration*, *The Option Trader's Workbook*, and *The Volatility Edge in Options Trading*. He currently teaches option trading classes at the New York Institute of Finance and writes a weekly column for *Stocks, Futures and Options* magazine.

Preface

Most investors who buy a stock believe that they are investing in a company. That view, while technically correct, is also misleading. A stock investment is really nothing more than a bet on the direction that money will take as it flows through the financial markets. A stock can rise only if market forces align to aggressively drive up the bid price causing new money to flow into the stock.

Many different factors are involved including economic news, announcements from other companies in the same industry, political events, the actions of large institutional investors, analysts' forecasts, and a variety of global economic forces such as changes to currency exchange rates and interest rates. The long-term performance of a stock represents nothing more than the compounded effect of these forces over time.

It is also important to recognize that the financial markets are a zero sum game with competition at all levels. The stock market competes for money against the bond and currency markets; industries compete for money with each other; and money flows between stocks within a particular industry. An individual stock can fall because money is flowing into the bond market. It can also fall because money is flowing into another stock in the same industry. Conversely, the stock of a poorly performing company can rise if market forces are properly aligned. All factors considered, the price of a stock is often only loosely connected to the performance of the underlying company.

There was a time, not long ago, when individual investors were the dominant force in the market. Buying a stock was equivalent to betting on the behavior of the other market participants. Those days have passed. Today's markets react to economic news in a fraction of a second, with computer algorithms driving most of the behavior. Heavily traded stocks in the S&P 100 or Dow rise and fall for reasons that are nearly impossible to understand at the individual stock level.

Investors who recognize these complex dynamics can gain an advantage because they have a balanced, realistic view of the problem. They spend most of their time identifying the underlying forces driving the markets, and they always try to invest with those forces instead of against them. In this regard, the most important attribute an investor can have is humbleness because successful investing is a never-ending struggle. The goal of this book is to make that struggle easier.

First Principles

This book is designed to help investors understand the economic and political forces that drive financial markets and to invest *alongside* those forces instead of *against* them. It also provides a blunt assessment of the limitations that most private investors face. Understanding these limitations and being able to manage risk are as important as choosing the right investments.

The following basic principles are central to the theme of this book:

- Financial markets, and stock markets in particular, always move in the direction that will do the most damage to the most investors. There are valid mathematical reasons underlying this assertion. In the most basic terms, when a large number of investors are on one side of the market and the market moves against them, the short-term losses create a wave of activity that becomes self-reinforcing. It is for this very reason that high-volume days with the most aggressive buying tend to occur just before sharp corrections.

- Financial markets are interrelated. Understanding the effects of one market on another is critical to successful investing. Nobody should ever invest in a market that doesn't make sense to them. In this regard, it is critical to be able to rationalize moves of the market with changes in the economy and financial news.
- Individual stocks tend to be swept along by the market. Even the best companies suffer declines during a market correction, and the worst companies can rally in a strong bull market. The gap between market and individual stock performance is not always obvious.
- Many investors blame the market when their stocks decline and credit themselves with wise investing when the same stocks rise. They never take the opposite view—that is, they never believe that they're lucky when they make money and that their losses are due to bad investment decisions. Taking a more pessimistic view will make you a better investor. It will drive you to work harder and be more diligent. Blame yourself, not the market, for losses.
- Experienced investors tend to overrate their knowledge about the companies they invest in. Gaining insights not already known to the market is a very difficult undertaking. Quarterly reports and analyst reviews cannot fill the gap. If you can't describe a company in terms of its revenue streams, sales pipelines, distribution channels, product roadmaps, and business models, then you don't understand the

company well enough to become a shareholder. Recognize that buying shares of stock is equivalent to purchasing a minority stake in a company. Don't invest in a company that you wouldn't feel comfortable owning, and if you can't gain that level of comfort then don't invest.

- The ability to interpret and understand government reports and news releases is a critical skill. These reports contain a wealth of information buried at a level of detail that most investors try to avoid. It is a mistake to let the financial news media interpret this information for you. Complexity and detail are your friends because they allow you to gain an advantage over the market and lazy investors who are unwilling to do their own homework.
- Understanding and avoiding risk is a key component of basic investing. Understand the relative risks of different financial instruments and avoid overusing leverage. Don't be fooled into believing that interest-earning investments are automatically safe. The most dangerous three words in the investment world are "can't possibly happen."

These concepts will weigh heavily in our discussions. However, they are not intended as simple guidelines and, on their own, they cannot be used to choose profitable trades. They are intended as background themes that can be used to guide your thinking.

Chapter 1

Global Economic Forces and the Average Investor

Trade Imbalances, Fiscal Policy, and the Average Investor

In 2005, someone asked me what I thought the best investment was. "Short the U.S. dollar or buy gold," I responded—an unusual statement for an option trader. When I spoke those words, gold traded at $450 per ounce. Four years later, at the time of this writing, gold was worth $1,150. The prediction was based on a couple of simple financial dynamics. In 2005, the world's combined gross domestic product (GDP) was around $45 trillion, but the U.S. trade deficit had ballooned to $800 billion. Interest rates around the globe had already collapsed into a range of 1%–2%. Simply multiplying these numbers revealed that the U.S. trade deficit was consuming an amount of money equal to all the risk-free interest earned in the world (2% of $45 trillion is $900 billion). The situation had become unsustainable and the trade deficit was destined to unwind. Moreover, every conceivable mechanism for unwinding the trade imbalance involved a weaker dollar and a substantial increase in the money supply. The trade deficit problem was further compounded by the cost of the Iraq and Afghanistan wars, which were also consuming massive amounts of cash. The simple end result would almost certainly be a sharp increase in the price of gold as it is priced in dollars.

That prediction turned out to be better than I had expected. The government went on a wild money printing binge, and by March 2006, the problem had become so severe that they stopped reporting the M3 money supply number.[1] The dollar continued to plunge, and we eventually reached a point where the British pound was worth $2.00, the euro $1.57, and the Japanese yen $1.15. By 2008, everyone was buying gold; there were even television commercials about gold.

So why did most investors and financial advisors miss this opportunity? The answer lies in the deceptive complexity of the analysis. Most investors have no idea what worldwide GDP is, and very few track the trade deficit—the two most significant components of this discussion. The concept of "risk-free" rate of return is also unfamiliar to most, as are the mechanisms by which the money supply is regulated. Where exactly does the money come from to fight a war? How does the U.S. government finance the trade deficit? Why does a weaker dollar help reduce the imbalance? How is gold priced in different currencies and when does its price move independently? What is the relationship between the federal funds rate, the typical interest rates paid by borrowers, and the risk-free rate of return? Most important of all, how does a weak dollar affect foreign investors who buy U.S. treasuries, and how does the money from these investments flow through the economy? The answers to these and many other questions form the underlying basis for understanding the trade imbalance.

All the facts were readily available, but linking them together into a macro-level picture is never easy. Very few investors—or academic economists, for that matter—pay close attention to the underlying components of the trade deficit. Few realize, for example, that the imbalance is further exaggerated by differences in import-export content between nations. The U.S. tends to import manufactured products—cars, televisions, clothing—in addition to its largest import, crude oil. In return, it exports technology and less tangible products such as credit derivatives. Virtually nobody in the investment community during the early 2000s mentioned that complex banking products, including the infamous credit default swaps that ruined the banking system in 2008, were counted in the trade balance as a significant American export. In 2005, with the trade deficit approaching $800 billion, the major exports of the U.S. were dollars and jobs.

In practical terms, the trade deficit became unsustainable because other countries—namely China—were lending the U.S. hundreds of billions of dollars each year to buy their products. The flow of money is always key to understanding the dynamics of any financial environment. In this case, dollars were flowing out of the U.S. to purchase foreign products. These dollars accumulated in foreign countries and were eventually lent back to the U.S. through the purchase of Treasury bonds, fixed-income securities sold directly by the government. The money worked its way through the banking system and ended up back in the hands of American citizens who continued borrowing and purchasing foreign products.

The same dollars went around and around in a never-ending circle, with U.S. debt accumulating in the hands of foreign countries and foreign products piling up in American households.

Another important dynamic, the one that ultimately hammered the final nail in the dollar's coffin, was the selection of a Federal Reserve Chairman with a long history of support for "re-inflation" strategies. Ben Bernanke replaced Alan Greenspan as Chairman of the Board of Governors of the Federal Reserve System and the system's monetary policymaking body, the Federal Open Market Committee, on February 1, 2006. His academic background includes a large number of research papers and books describing the benefits of "printing money." In a now-famous 2002 speech, Bernanke stated:

> Like gold, U.S. dollars have value only to the extent that they are strictly limited in supply. But the U.S. government has a technology, called a printing press (or, today, its electronic equivalent), that allows it to produce as many U.S. dollars as it wishes at essentially no cost. By increasing the number of U.S. dollars in circulation, or even by credibly threatening to do so, the U.S. government can also reduce the value of a dollar in terms of goods and services, which is equivalent to raising the prices in dollars of those goods and services. We conclude that, under a paper-money system, a determined government can always generate higher spending and hence positive inflation.[2]

No statement could ever have been more foretelling of fiscal policy. By February 2006, we had a runaway trade imbalance and a Federal Reserve Chairman who had already articulated an inflationary strategy for addressing the problem by weakening the dollar to reduce the cost of American products for overseas buyers and increase the cost of foreign products for Americans. Wise investors recognizing gold's history as a hedge against inflation bought gold—they were essentially betting with the house. For many of the same reasons, they also bought oil and other commodities, stocks, and bonds. Each of these markets skyrocketed on the power of a weakening dollar. Stocks became less expensive to foreign investors and the stock market climbed, bonds rallied as interest rates fell, and oil prices shot up from $55 per barrel in February 2006 to $140 during the summer of 2008. Oil was especially interesting because its price was driven by increased demand from a booming economy stimulated by low interest rates in addition to the effect of a weaker dollar. Speculators who recognized the trend jumped in and pushed prices even higher.

Strong Dollar, Weak Stock Market

Recent history reveals the importance of delving beyond the superficial levels of information presented in most articles and television interviews. The key point is that insight into the world's financial markets is often more valuable than any particular trading strategy. A good rule to follow is to stay out of the market if you cannot explain the changes using basic financial principles. We will return to this concept over and over again because it is the basic premise of this book. The market is not random and changes to the market always happen for a reason. For example, during the 2005–2009 time frame, the market often rallied on negative financial news. Bearish investors with short positions were often frustrated; many went broke continually betting against the market while it continued to rally. For a while, it seemed that the market behaved irrationally, because each piece of negative news resulted in a rally. Headlines added to the confusion with statements like "Wall Street Shrugs Off Job Losses." Savvy investors understood that Wall Street wasn't "shrugging off" anything. They understood that negative news weakened the dollar, further fueling the rally by reducing the prices of U.S. stocks for foreign investors. They also understood, however, that certain types of extremely negative news could have the opposite effect by reducing demand for products or services or by increasing the savings rate and taking dollars out of circulation. The best investors succeed because they know how to walk this fine line.

An important standard indicator that helps investors measure the relative strength of the U.S. dollar is the dollar index. The index is based on a weighted basket of currencies as follows:

Euro	57.0%
Yen (Japan)	13.6%
Pound (U.K.)	11.9%
Dollar (Canada)	9.1%
Krona (Sweden)	4.2%
Franc (Switzerland)	3.6%

Figure 1.1 displays the dollar index beginning the week of Ben Bernanke's appointment as Federal Reserve Chairman and ending at the low point of the dollar's decline 28 months later.

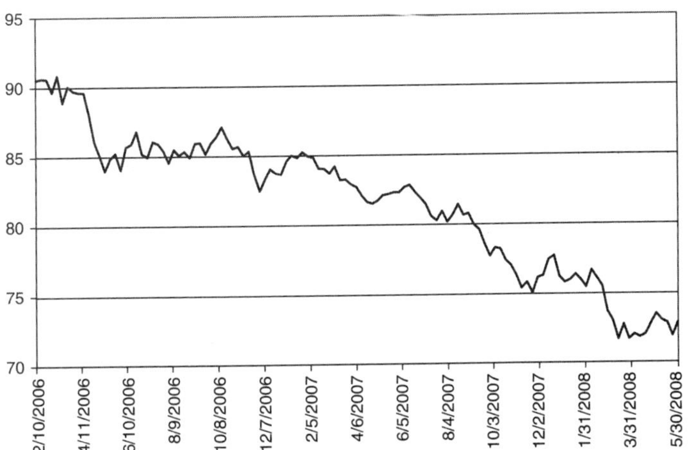

FIGURE 1.1 *Dollar index 2/10/2006–5/30/2008. U.S. fiscal policy and the resulting dollar collapse were key driving forces in global financial markets during this time frame.*

The index has become increasingly important for both long- and short-term investing. A strong inverse relationship between the relative strength of the dollar and the stock market is evident in long-term charts of the broad market. Figure 1.2 illustrates this point by comparing weekly values for the SPDR Trust (SPY) and the dollar index (DXY) from February 2006 through November 2009. SPY is displayed on the left *y*-axis (light gray line); DXY is displayed on the right *y*-axis (dark line).

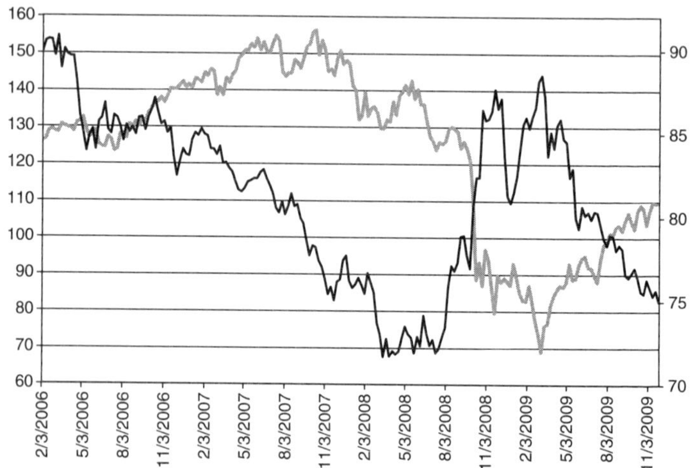

FIGURE 1.2 *Weekly chart of dollar index (DXY) versus SPDR Trust (SPY) February 2006 through November 2009. SPY is displayed on the left y-axis (light gray line); DXY is displayed on the right y-axis (dark line). Closing dates appear on the x-axis.*

The correlation between dollar weakness and stock market strength persisted through both good and bad financial times. It even transcended the 2008 banking collapse and a 50% drawdown in the stock market. Surprisingly, the dollar strengthened during the second half of 2008; a stronger dollar during this time frame was consistent with continued collapse of the market as it increased the relative price of U.S. investments for the rest of the world. This dynamic helped to accelerate the collapse, which ended when the dollar began to weaken again in March 2009.

Like any financial correlation, the dollar/stock relationship displayed in Figure 1.2 is somewhat imprecise. The strength of the correlation varies over time and is highly dependent on a variety of market conditions. For example, when the housing bubble began to reach unprecedented proportions and the long rally began to sputter, the market leveled off and stopped responding to the weak dollar. Between February 8 and March 14, the S&P 500 fell 3% despite a 6.5% drop in dollar index. The correlation strengthened again after the downward market correction ended, and by mid-2009, the behavior of the market was once again heavily dependent on the dollar. Figure 1.3, which charts the falling dollar against the rising market during the second half of 2009, confirms that the correlation was back in full force.

FIGURE 1.3 *Dollar index (DXY) versus SPDR Trust (SPY) July–December 2009. SPY is displayed on the left y-axis (light gray line); DXY is displayed on the right y-axis (dark line). Closing dates appear on the x-axis.*

As always, the dynamics were complex. The return of the weak dollar/strong stock market relationship contains valuable lessons for investors in all markets. It began in July 2009 as many traders started to question the rally, which seemed to have a life of its own. The economy remained weak and top-line revenue for most large corporations was continuing to shrink. Yet the market had rallied 32% with no hint of a reversal. Bearish investors had suffered severe losses, as each downward correction was immediately followed by a strong rally. They stopped launching short positions and waited on the sidelines. At the same time, bullish investors became increasingly cautious about a rally that was difficult to justify on economic grounds and had not experienced a single significant correction. A weak economy coupled with ultra-low emergency-level interest rates designed to provide stimulus was creating an environment that was difficult to understand. Both bullish and bearish investors began avoiding risk by trading in very short time frames.

A new trade emerged to dominate the market. Investors borrowed U.S. dollars at extremely low interest rates and invested the money in a variety of financial instruments. They were profiting from the small difference between the cost of borrowing dollars and the value they could obtain elsewhere. Each time the dollar strengthened—even slightly—the same investors closed their trades and paid back their loans. When the dollar weakened, money poured back into the markets. Because the transactions are made electronically, the effect is immediate. This type of trade, commonly referred to as a "carry" trade, dominated the U.S. stock market from July 2008 until the dollar was finally viewed as oversold by many foreign exchange traders in December 2009. During this time frame, minute-by-minute charts of the dollar became one of the most important technical indicators for traders in all financial markets. Whether they knew it or not, all investors were currency traders during this time frame.

Minute-by-minute carry trade effects are clearly visible in Figure 1.4, which charts the dollar against the S&P 500 on November 27, 2009. The light gray line in the figure traces the value of the SPDR Trust (SPY) and the dark line traces the dollar index (DXY). Time is displayed on the *x*-axis. The lines are virtual mirror images of each other. Each move of the dollar, no matter how small, is met with an immediate move of the market in the opposite direction. The effect is so powerful that it causes the market to exaggerate many of the smaller changes.

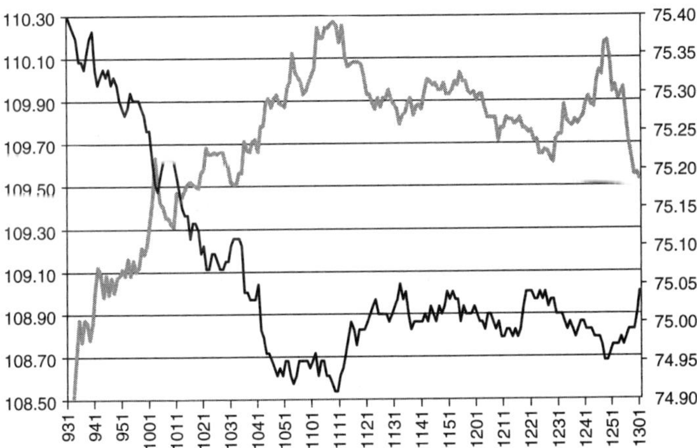

FIGURE 1.4 *Minute-by-minute prices for the SPDR Trust (SPY) and the dollar index (DXY) on 11/27/2009. SPY is displayed on the left y-axis (light gray line); DXY is displayed on the right y-axis (dark line). Time is displayed on the x-axis.*

November 27 was a particularly stringent test of the principle because it was a shortened trading day for the U.S. equity markets with no scheduled financial news for the dollar to react to. In addition, trading volume was exceptionally light; carry trade effects are much stronger on heavily traded days with important financial news. During this time frame, the vast majority of investors made their trading decisions without ever realizing that the moment-by-moment value of the U.S. dollar was the overwhelming force driving the markets. Successful investors understood these dynamics, and their decisions were based on forward-looking views of the foreign exchange markets. They chose investments that benefited from a weak dollar, but more importantly, they were quick to exit these trades when the dollar appeared to be oversold.

Currency effects can also create self-correcting forces that prevent the stock market from rising or falling. During the second half of 2009, when the carry trade was a powerful force, negative financial news often resulted in a falling dollar that created market stimulus. This stimulus effectively offset the effect of the bad news and caused the market to rally. Conversely, positive news that strengthened the dollar prevented the market from experiencing the rally that would have occurred if the news alone drove the market. Investors were often surprised when negative news caused the market to rise or positive news resulted in a decline. Generally speaking, it is a good idea to avoid investing if you cannot explain the market's response to financial news.

Foreign exchange rates have other important implications. Very few American investors, regardless of their level of expertise, value their returns in constant dollars—a mistake that is uncommon in the European or Asian investing communities. Foreign investors in U.S. markets tend to calculate their returns in their native currency. These calculations automatically correct for weakening or strengthening of the dollar. Figure 1.5 illustrates this concept by charting the S&P 500 in constant dollars and comparing to the native index. The upper line in the figure (light gray) displays the value of the index; the lower line displays the adjusted value in euros. Both traces span the time frame from early March 2009 through the end of the year. The difference is striking. European investors buying the S&P 500 in euros would have experienced a much smaller rally than American investors trading in U.S. dollars. But they also avoided the damaging effects of currency devaluation.

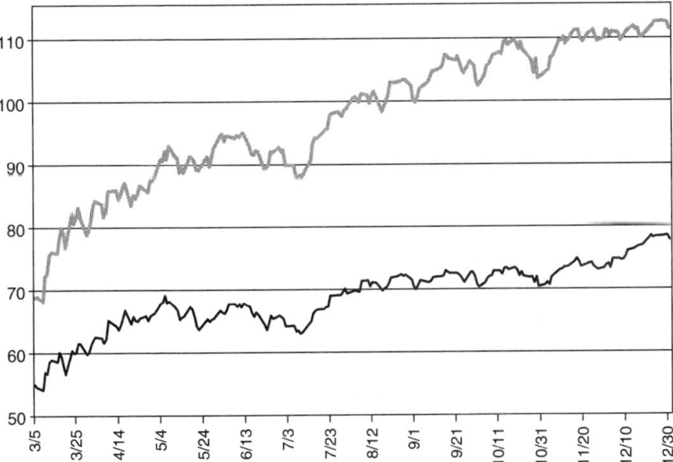

FIGURE 1.5 *Comparison of the SPDR Trust (SPY) priced in dollars (light gray line), and the same index priced in euros (dark line), 3/5/2009–12/31/2009.*

These dynamics have been played out many times during the past several years. Unfortunately, the vast majority of investors have fallen victim to the misconception that they had wisely chosen their investments and were making money, when, in fact, they were barely breaking even or losing to currency devaluation. Figure 1.6 displays one of the worst examples.

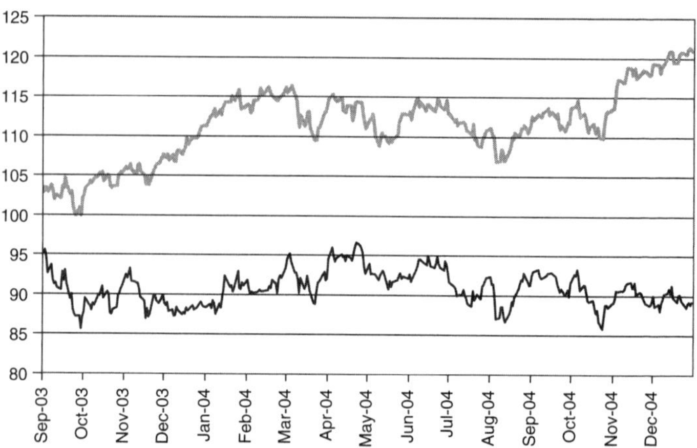

FIGURE 1.6 *Comparison of the SPDR Trust (SPY) priced in dollars (light gray line) and in euros (dark line), 9/1/2003–12/31/2004.*

During the 16 months displayed, the SPDR Trust climbed 18% in U.S. dollars but fell 6% in euros. American investors who invested in the broad market during this time frame falsely believed that they had realized a profit; European investors knew better. The difference, 24%, is the amount of profit that U.S. investors needed to generate just to break even. Stated differently, an 18% gain in the S&P 500 resulted in a

6% loss when the score was tabulated in dollars. Only investors who truly understood and could leverage the forces driving the dollar succeeded during this time frame. They invested in stocks that benefited from a weak dollar. However, as we shall see, this approach is fraught with risk because predicting the effects of currency exchange rates on most companies is much more complex than it might appear. Many stock analysts, for example, predicted that Hewlett-Packard would benefit from the weak dollar because it would reduce their prices in the worldwide market. They were wrong. The stock began and ended the time frame depicted in Figure 1.6 at the same price. The situation was much more complex than it appeared because it involved an understanding of the company's underlying model for managing money, paying taxes around the world, international labor costs, tariffs, material costs, and so on. Superimposed on all this complexity is a hedging operation—large companies normally engage in foreign exchange trading to offset the effects of varying exchange rates. Unfortunately, these trading operations can become a source of risk when the forex (foreign exchange) markets move in surprising ways. Betting on a large multinational corporation during a time frame dominated by large swings in the forex market is equivalent to betting on their ability to manage exchange rates. Companies with a strong history of success in the forex markets are the best investment candidates under these circumstances.

This discussion is intended to highlight the extent to which global economic forces affect individual investments. The effect is especially relevant to stock investors who are often surprised when seemingly solid investments lose money as they fail to keep pace with currency devaluation. Worse still, most investors don't understand the impact of a high beta portfolio. Beta is a measure of the tendency of a security's returns to respond to swings of the market. Stocks with high beta values exaggerate changes in the market; low beta stocks dampen the changes. A stock with a beta of 1.5 will be 50% more volatile than the market. Stock investors often make the mistake of structuring a high beta portfolio without recognizing the risk. When their portfolio outperforms a rising market, they mistakenly believe that they have chosen superior stocks that will continue to outperform. Unfortunately, when the market declines, their portfolio falls faster. In the end, they usually believe that their mistake was not closing everything and taking profit at the top of the rally. The real mistake, however, was not hedging against the high beta character of the portfolio with trades that would generate profit if the market declined. This mistake has been exacerbated in recent years by the availability of exchange traded funds (ETFs) that are designed to exaggerate the behavior of the market they represent. Today's choices include 2X and 3X ETFs in commodities, energy, banking, retail, and just about any area that an investor chooses to focus on. These funds are often referred to as "double long," "triple long," "double short," or "triple short." While they can be excellent vehicles for capitalizing on a trend, they are also the epitome of high beta that needs to be hedged.

Endnotes

1. Three different money supply numbers are calculated. The most restrictive, M1, is limited to currency in the hands of the public. It includes travelers checks, demand deposits (checking accounts), and other deposits against which checks can be written. M2 includes all of M1, plus savings accounts, time deposits of under $100,000, and balances in retail money market mutual funds. M3 is the broadest measure. It includes all of M1 and M2 plus large-denomination ($100,000 or more) time deposits, balances in institutional money funds, repurchase liabilities issued by depository institutions, and eurodollars held by U.S. residents at foreign branches of U.S. banks and banks in the United Kingdom and Canada.

2. Remarks by Gov. Ben S. Bernanke before the National Economists Club, Washington, D.C., 21 November 2002.

Chapter 2

The Harsh Realities of the Marketplace

Identifying Critical Information

Understanding the effects of global economic forces on the stock market is just one piece of a large and complex puzzle. Purchasing individual stocks requires true insight into the finances of individual companies. These insights are not easy to come by. Consequently, investors rarely understand the risks they take. During every moment of every trading day, a relatively cautious and otherwise conservative person clicks their mouse and purchases shares of a well known stock like Apple, IBM, or Google whether they know anything about the company or not. Someone, for example, who buys 200 shares of Apple Computer is making a decision to spend tens of thousands of dollars ($44,000 at the time of this writing). Ask that person if they can name some of Apple's largest customers, most important suppliers, major competitors, describe their product roadmap, identify their various revenue streams, or if they have any knowledge of the state of their sales pipelines, and they are likely to respond with a blank expression. In short—they know virtually nothing about the company.

Investors who buy stocks should try to behave more like venture capitalists (VCs). Most VCs are absolutely relentless in their pursuit of detailed knowledge about a potential investment. They spend weeks meeting with company executives, customers, suppliers, business partners, and outside consultants who can provide expert opinions on the business. No stone is left unturned. By the time VCs decide to invest, they know absolutely everything that can be known about a company. But more importantly, their investments are structured with anti-dilution clauses that provide protection against the effects of large infusions of new capital from future investors. This structure allows a company to bring in additional growth capital while protecting the financial interests of the original owners. Finally, virtually all VCs secure a liquidation preference that places them ahead of everyone else—even the CEO—if the company is dissolved or sold. In short, they spend significant amounts of time and money to understand every nuance of the business before investing. Then when they finally invest, they structure the deal to include as much downside protection as possible. But even more significant is the actual source of the money which, in most cases, is a group of high net worth individuals who have invested in the VC's portfolio of startup companies. All factors considered, most VCs can better afford a significant loss than a typical private investor.

The contrast is shocking. A typical private investor with a relatively small tolerance for loss will often spend a proportionately larger amount of his net worth on an investment than an experienced venture capitalist. Most people spend more time researching the purchase of a car than a stock—even though a stock investment can easily be more expensive and can lose money much more quickly. They don't understand that quarterly earnings reports, analyst reviews, and detailed knowledge about specific industries are all comprehended by the market and already priced into the stock. A thorough grasp of all this information still does not place a private investor on par with Wall Street analysts who have direct access to company executives in the form of private briefings and question-and-answer sessions. Large institutions that buy stocks conduct the same level of due diligence as a venture capitalist.

Before making an investment, it is important to ask the following questions: "What do I know that the market doesn't; what information do I have that is not already comprehended in the price?" Unless the answers are clear and concise, the investment is a mistake. Following this guideline will force you to delve into the workings of a company to gain meaningful insights that transcend traditional views of the market. In the final analysis, these skills are the most valuable a private investor can have.

Meaningful Insights and Unique Views

Meaningful insight into a company's business is always difficult to obtain. The details are often surprising. Consider, for example, IBM—a widely followed, heavily traded blue-chip stock. Most investors are unaware that many of IBM's largest customers are also direct competitors—a major risk factor for the business. The conflict was especially strong during the late 1990s and early 2000s when sales of microprocessors, disk drives, storage systems, and other electronic hardware were the company's primary focus. Because very few private investors knew that Apple was one of IBM's largest customers, the impact of Apple's decision to switch its platform from the IBM Power architecture to Intel in 2006 went mostly unnoticed by the investment community. That decision had far-reaching implications, not the least of which is the requirement for a chip-fabrication plant to achieve a minimum number of "wafer starts" each day to remain efficient. Falling below this threshold can cause the business to become uncompetitive. In IBM's case, it also posed a risk to the mainframe business, which was based on the same chip architecture as Apple's computers at the time. Apple's processor volume was important to IBM's mainframe business.

Most investors are also unaware of the importance of IBM's technology licensing business, which is built on the company's patent portfolio. According to IBM's Web site, the company received more than 38,000 U.S. patents between 1993 and 2007. Since 1996, the company has invested approximately $5 billion each year in research and development. Investing in IBM without understanding this particular money flow is dangerous because intellectual property licensing is a major revenue stream for the company. It has many complexities, ranging from cross-licensing agreements with other technology companies to patent exposure from participation in open source software development where technology is freely licensed to the public.

Finally, IBM realizes a large amount of revenue from interest on loans made to customers. Much of the money for these loans comes from selling bonds. Stated differently, the company borrows money and then lends the borrowed money to customers at higher interest rates than it pays. The customers use this money to buy IBM products and services. Profit is made on the arbitrage between IBM's cost of money and the interest paid by customers, in addition to the profits earned from selling products to customers who might otherwise not be able to afford them. These financial transactions add complexity to both the underlying business and its financial reporting. Most significantly, there's the business of lending customers money so they can buy products—a process that is far from riskless. Suppose, for example, that a financially troubled customer goes out of business after purchasing equipment with borrowed money. In such circumstances, the lender is likely to lose both the money and the cost of the equipment. Moreover, lending money involves analyzing credit, structuring loan agreements, and tracking collections—not exactly core competencies for most computer companies.

While a complete discussion of these issues as they apply to IBM is beyond the scope of this book, one thing is clear: Most stockholders do not fully comprehend the business in which they have invested. They have no idea that technology licensing is one of the company's most profitable revenue streams, that some of the largest customers are major competitors, and that banking operations are a major source of revenue. Layer on multibillion-dollar stock buybacks, currency trading, and a complex model for paying taxes internationally, and the complexity grows beyond the reach of most investors and, surprisingly, most analysts. Unfortunately, people who buy the stock without a firm understanding of these issues are just throwing investment money at something they don't understand.

In broad terms, one might say that it is often difficult to understand the real business that a company is focused on. Intel, for example, generated a large amount of profit from its venture capital arm during the late 1990s. Unfortunately, the street assigned a lower price/earnings (PE) ratio to this type of business, and the stock suffered despite strong earnings. This particular problem often plagues a company when it finds new and innovative sources of revenue. Sometimes the transition is not so obvious. McDonalds, for example, effectively entered the toy business in 1979 when it introduced the Happy Meal for children. Each Happy Meal bundled a small amount of food, a drink, and a toy. Since 1979, the offerings have been expanded to include a version for older children, the Mighty Kid's Meal, and a variety of special promotions. The toys have also become more elaborate; many are related to an existing toy line or contemporary motion picture. In effect, the company is selling toys and including a small amount of food for free. This view is driven by the fact that the toy is the attraction—especially for very young children. Happy Meals, therefore, should be marketed as toys, not food.

Swimming Upstream

Investors also tend to make the mistake of trading large-cap stocks that are the focus of large institutional traders. Statistics show that investors who focus on heavily traded stocks have a worse record than investors who avoid these stocks. The reason for the disadvantage is that the market is a zero sum game in which every dollar won must also be lost. Investors who trade large-cap stocks—let's say IBM or Google—are pitting themselves against institutional traders with much more information and direct access to the companies they invest in. A private investor cannot win that game.

This problem came sharply into focus in early January 2010 when Goldman Sachs admitted to trading ahead of and sometimes against its own clients, with information that gave the company a decided advantage. In one situation, Goldman Sachs sold bundles of mortgages in the form of collateralized debt obligations to clients while, at the same time, shorting them in their own portfolio. The story broke when a senior executive sent an e-mail message to clients disclosing the conflict. The actual message is included in the endnotes for this chapter.[1]

The Goldman Sachs story took a new and shocking turn on April 16, 2010, when the company was accused of securities fraud in a civil suit filed by the Securities and Exchange Commission (SEC). The suit claimed that the bank had created and sold mortgage investments that were secretly designed to fail. The details were complex; they involved the investment activities of famous hedge fund manager John Paulson who was not directly accused of any wrongdoing by the SEC.[2]

After analyzing risky home mortgages in Arizona, California, Florida, and Nevada, Mr. Paulson approached Goldman Sachs to discuss betting against those loans. His analysis, which focused on adjustable-rate mortgages secured by borrowers with relatively low credit scores, turned up more than 100 loan pools that he considered vulnerable. According to the SEC, Paulson asked Goldman Sachs to assemble a portfolio of these pools that he could wager against. The discussions resulted in the creation of a new debt security known as ABACUS 2007-AC1. According to the complaint, Paulson & Co. paid Goldman Sachs approximately $15 million for structuring and marketing ABACUS. The deal closed on April 26, 2007; by October 24, 83% of the loans in the portfolio had been downgraded and 17% were on negative watch. By January 29, 2008, 99% of the portfolio had been downgraded.

As the value of ABACUS collapsed, Paulson's negative bet made huge sums of money while investors who were sold the other side of the trade lost more than $1 billion. Worse still, Goldman Sachs led its customers to believe that all the investments were selected by ACA Management, LLC, a third party with experience analyzing credit risk for residential mortgage-backed securities (RMBS). John Paulson's role in selecting and betting against the portfolio contents was completely hidden. ACA was also misled—they were told that

Paulson had invested $200 million in the equity of ABACUS, when, in fact, his investments were designed to profit from its collapse. It's safe to say that none of Goldman Sachs's customers would have put money into an investment that was carefully designed to fail—especially when the fund manager who chose the portfolio contents was betting on the failure. ABACUS, while the focus of the SEC's case, was one of 25 deals that Goldman created so the bank and select clients could bet against the housing market.[3]

The Goldman Sachs case is complex and, at the time of this writing, it was still unresolved. The company asserts that it did nothing wrong, and many legal and financial experts agree. Although this book is certainly not the proper forum for voicing opinions on the merits of the SEC's accusations, the situation brings a few important principles sharply into focus:

- First and most important is the recognition that someone must always take the other side of every trade. If there were no counterparty, there would be no market and the trade would not exist.
- Second: Always assume that the party on the other side knows at least as much as you do.
- Third: Whether the party on the other side is a large investment bank, a successful hedge fund, your neighbor, the world's most successful investor, or someone living under a bridge should make absolutely no difference. You should always make investment decisions based on thorough research and your own understanding of the market.

- Fourth: Knowing who the counterparty is does not provide any information about that party's opinion. A significant long position might be part of a more complex multipart trade that is net short. Stated differently, the long or short position you are aware of might really be a hedge against a larger position on the opposite side of the market.

The kind of behavior alleged in the SEC's lawsuit can manifest itself in many different ways. It's normally less overt and more difficult to define than the ABACUS debacle. In most cases, knowledgeable investors with inside information about an event simply win in the marketplace against outsiders not privy to the same information. I have a friend who directly experienced the real-life impact of this sort of behavior. He's an experienced professional trader at a large investment bank. In June 2009, after a considerable amount of research, he opened a significant long position on Google, with the stock trading around $425. His reasons were solid enough. They included growth and expansion forecasts in Asia, strong advertising revenue, and a variety of positive financial forecasts revealed by the company at an analyst briefing. On July 1, the stock reached a high of $426.40 before retreating to $418.99. Something was definitely wrong. July 2 was worse; the stock fell to $406.49. More shocking than the monetary loss was the lack of information that could explain the drawdown. On July 7, after just one week, the stock fell below $396 and my friend closed his position, realizing a $30 loss. Only three days later, on July 10, Goldman Sachs issued an upgrade for Google and the stock began rising quickly. By July 16, the stock traded as high as $445.75.

The lesson is clear: Someone who did all the right research, reached the right conclusion, and bought the stock a couple of weeks ahead of the crowd lost a huge amount of money because his timing was out of sync with the upgrade. Even worse, the predictions made in the upgrade were exactly the same as his. He was penalized for good foresight. Why the stock fell so sharply in the days leading up to the upgrade is anybody's guess. A suspicious person would say that someone who knew about the report in advance spread rumors and took action to drive down the price so he could buy in just ahead of the positive news. There's no way to know for sure, but it certainly happens often enough to create a huge capability gap between large, powerful financial institutions and everyone else.

Many will respond that "long-term investing" is the answer. They will argue that Google ultimately rallied, and that it remained an excellent investment until January 2010, when the stock peaked out at more than $625 per share. Unfortunately, this peak was immediately followed by a sharp decline that took the price down more than $100 in just 17 days. During the steep rally, Google outperformed the market, and during the decline, it fell much faster. Long-term investors also weathered interim storms that took the stock down 4% to 5% in a few days. A strong sell-off of a stock that is heavily traded by large institutions is always significant. Taking the other side of the trade by trying to predict the bottom is always dangerous. Generally speaking, it is dangerous to play in a game that someone else controls. Trading large-cap stocks is such a game.

The "Long Term" Fallacy

"Long-term investing" is a relic from a previous era when constant, steady growth was common at all levels in the economy. The natural course of events was for small companies to grow into large ones, and for large corporations to "globalize" and become part of the expanding world economy. Growth rates in the United States were spectacular from the end of the Vietnam War until the NASDAQ collapse in 2000. Most investors made the mistake of believing that they made money because they knew what they were doing. In reality, they made money because they were swept along by a robust economy. Even poorly run companies profited, and the ones that failed were usually acquired, often for outrageous sums of money. Long-term investing is easy when the winners grow exponentially and the losers are acquired by the winners.

Those days are gone forever; the numbers don't lie. At the beginning of 1990, before the internet and biotech booms, the S&P 500 was priced at just 330. By 2000, it had rocketed to 1438. At the time of this writing, in 2010, the S&P was priced at 1100. So from early 2000 to early 2010, the market lost 24% of its value. This loss was further compounded by a 20% decline of the dollar index. Investors in U.S. markets effectively lost 40% of their money.

Many will argue that the market experienced large interim swings and that these changes represented outstanding investment opportunities. They are correct. The NASDAQ collapse bottomed out in 2003 with the S&P 500 at 851. It rallied back to the top (1540) in late 2007 and then fell to a new low (768) in 2009. The next rally, which stalled in early 2010, represented a 50% retracement from the low. "Long-term" investing is really nothing more than weathering these storms and hoping for the best. Stock pickers will always say that their stocks outperform the market. Even when they are right, there's a fallacy in this reasoning. Knowing how a company will perform over many years is simply not possible. Presumably, even the most bullish investor would sell a stock when presented with new information that contradicts his bullish view. Long-term investors are faced with this decision every day, whether they know it or not. Furthermore, most investors don't realize that deciding to hold a stock is exactly the same as deciding to buy it at the current price. There's absolutely no difference—buying and holding represent the same decision. Stated differently, you should never continue to hold a stock that you wouldn't purchase. Ignoring that fact is tantamount to blindly investing—over and over again—without ever revisiting the original decision. Investors who pursue this approach sometimes get lucky; they usually confuse luck with good investing. When they lose, they blame the market, the economy, or some other factor that they believe unfairly drove down the price of their stock. They usually believe that the drawdown is temporary and that it represents a new "buying opportunity." Unfortunately, they rarely recognize their own bad decision to hold a stock after the original reason for buying it has expired. Long-term investors always absorb losses with the hope that the stock will recover. Hoping and praying is a bad investment strategy, but it is the plight of the long-term investor.

The Fallacy of Paper Losses

The familiar term *paper loss* is most popular among long-term investors. It is frequently used to justify keeping a bad investment because closing it would convert the "paper loss" into a real loss. Roughly translated, it means: "I made a bad investment decision and lost money, but I am confident that over time that decision will prove to be correct."

Unfortunately paper losses are real losses, and they are reflected in the account balance. More importantly, holding onto a losing investment with the hope that it will turn around is unproductive because the money would provide more value invested in something moving in the right direction. The account has no way of knowing where each dollar comes from, and there is no particular reason that a loss needs to be recovered in its original investment. Money should always be deployed in an optimized way by selecting the most promising investments at any given moment. Hanging onto a losing position to avoid booking the loss makes no real sense, and it is often a very costly mistake. It, therefore, makes perfect sense to realize losses and move on, unless there are simply no better investments. Unfortunately, most stock investors also fool themselves into believing that they have already chosen the best trades.

Don't "Buy the Dips"

Long-term investors also frequently talk about "buying the dips." This approach combines and builds on the two concepts just discussed: long-term investing and paper losses. It's a flawed strategy created around the assumption that each drawdown represents some sort of market inefficiency that can be exploited for profit. As with many approaches, it also implies that the investor somehow knows more than the market. A better approach is to assume that the market is always right and that stock prices fall for a reason.

Strategies based on "buying the dips" also assume that it is possible to roughly estimate where the bottom is. Unfortunately, picking a bottom—or a top, for that matter—is extraordinarily difficult. The technical charting crowd always believes they can, but statistical evidence suggests otherwise. Despite claims too numerous to count, nobody has ever demonstrated a sure-fire reproducible method for calling the top or bottom of a short-term price change. Moreover, anyone who could accomplish that feat would be foolish to reveal the secret because the market would immediately extinguish the inefficiency that allowed the prediction.

There is no shortage of complex approaches to picking entry and exit points. Solutions range from simply buying and selling the stock as its price crosses a long-term moving average to using more complex algorithms that depend on moving averages in different time frames. One popular approach, for example, involves buying a stock when its 50-day moving average crosses its 200-day moving average on the way up, and selling when the two lines cross again on the way down.

Each of these approaches has its own problems. Simply buying and selling a stock as it crosses a single moving average is logistically impossible when successive up-and-down price changes around the moving average generate multiple buy and sell signals during a brief time frame. Unfortunately, this problem is the norm, not the exception, because stocks rarely move steadily in one direction. During congestion periods when the stock price remains relatively unchanged, the moving average and stock price will converge closely creating an impossible-to-trade situation. As a result, the indicator can only be used if some of the trading signals are ignored. Creating an indicator and deciding when to ignore it is a terrible approach to technical analysis.

Multiple moving averages and more complex combinations of indicators are the standard answer. They smooth out the noise and can provide new opportunities to identify features in a stock chart that might not be apparent to the unaided eye. However, technical charting, which can take the form of simple moving averages or complex statistical algorithms, is not an endeavor to be taken lightly. "Buying the dips" is not nearly as simple as it might seem. Bluntly stated, when a stock price falls sharply, it is generally better to close the investment and realize the loss than to keep the stock.

Misconceptions about Risk

Stock investors generally believe that purchasing a stock is a relatively conservative approach to investing. They rarely understand that there are many more conservative approaches to owning a stock that involve simple option positions. Most would be surprised to learn that long stock positions are riskier than long stock/short call (covered call) positions. The next step, known as a collar, is more conservative still. It consists of long stock, a short call, and a long put. Such positions limit both upside gains and downside risk. Few investors ever take advantage of these structures—even when the goal is to earn modest gains with limited risk. Surprisingly, these trade structures rarely appear in accounts controlled by professional money managers. Professionals find collars distasteful because, as mentioned earlier, the trade structure caps both the maximum gain and loss that can be realized. Such tradeoffs are insulting to people who believe that they can choose outstanding investments that consistently beat the market. The tradeoff also limits their ability to differentiate themselves from other money managers by generating outstanding returns. Unfortunately, the past decade has highlighted the fallacy in this thinking, as professional money managers have lost their clients billions of dollars in the stock market during financial meltdowns. The meltdowns weren't their fault, but the losses were. In virtually every instance, limiting the maximum loss and capping the potential gain would have been a superior strategy.

Although a detailed discussion of collars is beyond the scope of this book, a brief illustration should be helpful. An example might involve purchasing 100 shares of a $50 stock, selling a $55 strike price call, and using the proceeds from the sale to purchase a $45 strike price put. For simplicity, we will assume that the $55 call is at least as expensive as the $45 put. The trade, therefore, would cost slightly less than the stock purchase alone.

Let's assume that the stock trades for $60 on the day the option contracts expire. We would close our position by repurchasing the $55 call for $5 and keeping $10 profit in the stock. Our net profit would be capped at $5—the difference between the two sides of the trade. This cap would apply with the stock trading at any price above $55.

Alternatively, if the stock fell sharply to $30, we would realize a $15 profit from the $45 put and a $20 loss in the stock. Our net loss would be capped at $5, far better than the $20 loss that would have been realized in a simple "naked" long stock position. If we decided to keep the trade open, we would simply sell a new call—perhaps at the $35 strike—and buy a new put with the proceeds. No action would be required to close the trade since the broker would automatically exercise the profitable put by selling the stock at $45 (the strike price of the put contract). In trading terms, he would take advantage of our contract to "put" the stock to someone else at $45, despite the actual market price of $30.

Structuring the trade with current month options provides maximum flexibility because we can rebracket the stock with new options after each month's expiration. In this way, we would remain perpetually protected against sharp downturns in return for accepting a cap on our potential profits. With each trade, we could decide to widen or shrink the spacing between the strike prices to control the level of risk. In a strongly bullish market, we might decide to create a trade with wide spacing where the profit cap and downside protection were relatively small. Conversely, more narrow spacing would be appropriate in an unstable market where downside risk is high and we are willing to accept a tighter cap on our profits in return for more downside protection. In broad terms, collars are helpful for long-term investors because they make it possible to hold on to a losing trade and wait for the market to turn around. Limiting downside risk also facilitates structuring larger positions, another big advantage for many long-term investors.

The Perils of Earning Interest

Bond investors frequently underestimate risk. Many believe that they can safely earn interest regardless of what happens to the prices of the bonds they own. Unfortunately, when yields rise and bond prices fall, they end up effectively paying themselves the interest they were counting on because it is offset by principal losses in their account. The bond continues to pay its promised interest rate, while the underlying value declines. If interest rates rise high enough, the bond can become nearly worthless, forcing the holder to wait until maturity to retrieve the original investment. The value of an entire portfolio can collapse during inflationary periods marked by rising interest rates. Bonds can also become worthless during bad economic times when risk must be offset by rising yields. Such was the case during the 2008 banking collapse, when yields on corporate bonds doubled and tripled as rating agencies downgraded their debt. During this time frame, many bond investors decided to hold onto positions in financially insecure companies because they didn't want to sell their bonds at a loss. They felt comfortable earning the original interest rates and assumed that they could close their trades at some point in the future when rates returned to normal and the underlying bonds recovered their value. This approach often resulted in 100% losses when companies defaulted.

Second-guessing the bond market is as foolish as second-guessing the stock market. If a bond's rating falls and its interest rate rises, the risk has increased and the investment has lost money. It's not a "paper loss." It's not a "dip." It's not a "buying opportunity." It's a bad investment—period. This problem was made abundantly clear to me by a bond salesman who once declared that GM bonds were "a steal at 16% interest." He went on to say, "People are behaving like the company is going out of business. I'm putting all my clients in GM bonds." This conversation took place in early December 2008, after GM had already reported that it would run out of cash during the next six months without some combination of government funding, a merger, or sales of assets. I took the other side by stating that "GM is going out of business, and the bond market's pricing of its debt supports that view." We argued for a few minutes. He mentioned his vast experience in valuing companies and trading bonds. He also explained that GM was just bluffing. "They have enough cash to operate for the next two years," he explained. Not surprisingly, the market was right and he was wrong. Yields rose to even higher levels before the company finally declared bankruptcy.

Some investors, and irresponsible money managers, continually repeat this particular mistake because they believe they know something the market doesn't. In this regard, it is important to recognize that a bond that pays 16% interest is eight times riskier than a bond paying 2%. Not second-guessing this simple observation would have saved investors billions of dollars during the past few years.

Most public customers also don't understand that there are excellent hedged strategies for trading high-yield bonds. One strategy involves purchasing the bond while shorting the underlying stock. The short stock position serves as a hedge against default and collapse of the bonds. Suppose, for example, that an investor purchased $50,000 of high-yield bonds and shorted $50,000 of stock in a financially distressed company that ultimately collapsed into bankruptcy a year after the initial investment. During that year, the investor earned an unusually high rate of return, knowing all the time that the company might default. When the company collapsed, the stock became worthless and the short stock position delivered a $50,000 profit that completely offset the bond loss. The investor was able to benefit from an outstanding return while the company was solvent without ever worrying about the risk of default. In fact, the real risk for this trade was on the upside. If the company stabilized and the stock rallied, the short position might have lost more money than could be recovered by selling the bond. To avoid this problem, smart investors choose the very worst companies—ones that are unlikely to be acquired or bailed out by investors.

More than anything, this discussion is intended to highlight the sharp differences between a typical bond investor's approach to the market and that of a professional bond trader. The professional trader understands risk and earns money by exploiting and hedging price distortions. He makes mathematical decisions that depend as little as possible on opinions about the underlying company. The long bond/short stock trade is a perfect illustration because its underlying structure is designed around the notion that risk is underpriced and that the underlying company might actually default. Private investors take the opposite approach. They purchase a bond assuming that its interest rate fairly compensates them for the risk they are taking. Very few private bond investors hedge their purchases in a manner designed to fully offset, much less profit from, a 100% loss. In very real terms, they are playing a game that they don't understand. Worse still, because it's a zero sum game, the loser pays the winner. In this particular case, the loser might not even be aware of the loss for some time.

In blunt terms, bonds do not equal safety. Bonds are as risky as any other investment, and they should only be managed by investors who understand the underlying math that describes the relationships between risk, yield, and price. Few investors understand that purchasing a bond is exactly the same as lending money. Banks lend money. But banks are skilled at evaluating risk. An investor holding a portfolio of bonds is essentially a tiny independent bank without the necessary risk-assessment skills. The underlying assumption is always that rating agencies such as Standard and Poor's or Moody's have done their job and that the rating of a bond fairly represents its risk. This assumption has often turned out to be wrong, and the rating agencies have been heavily criticized for their mistakes.

In recent years, much damage has occurred in the accounts of retirees and others living on fixed incomes. In most cases, these individuals were steered toward "safe, interest-earning investments" that they believed were immune to large moves of the financial markets. This problem became especially acute during the 2008 banking collapse, when large, stable corporations were downgraded and interest rates on corporate bonds soared to levels more characteristic of junk bonds. Companies such as General Motors and Lehman Brothers, previously considered rock solid, defaulted on their bond issues and fell into bankruptcy. Others were forced to raise rates, destroying the value of previously issued debt instruments.

Finally, many investors who would otherwise have waited for the market to stabilize were swept up in the chaos and forced to sell because their trades were part of a larger portfolio being centrally managed by a financial institution. Wealthy investors often avoid this problem because their portfolio is the primary focus of a dedicated money manager who does not commingle their positions with other accounts. These investors have a distinct advantage, and the performance of their accounts significantly outpaces the average. They can also afford to absorb relatively large losses while waiting for the market to stabilize. Average investors who cannot afford to sustain substantial losses should not take advice from wealthy investors who have distinctly different risk profiles.

Endnotes

1. Andrew Ross Sorkin, "Goldman Acknowledges Conflicts with Clients," *DealBook, The New York Times,* 12 January 2010. http://dealbook.blogs.nytimes.com/2010/01/12/goldman-executive-discloses-conflicts-policy.

   Dear client,

   We may from time to time discuss with you Trading Ideas generated by our Fundamental Strategies Group. As part of our commitment to managing conflicts of interest appropriately, this message is to explain how the Fundamental Strategies Group interacts with other parts of our organisation and how that impacts on the Trading Ideas.

   The Fundamental Strategies Group is a group of cross-capital structure desk analysts employed by our Securities Divisions to assist our traders. They develop Trading Ideas in conjunction with traders. We may trade, and may have existing positions, based on Trading Ideas before we have discussed those Trading Ideas with you. We may continue to act on Trading Ideas, and may trade out of any position, based on Trading Ideas, at any time after we have discussed them with you. We will also discuss Trading Ideas with other clients, both before and after we have discussed them with you.

   You should not consider Trading Ideas as objective or independent research or as investment advice. When we discuss Trading Ideas with you, we will not be acting as your advisor (including, without limitation, in relation to investment, accounting, tax or legal matters) and the provision of Trading Ideas to you will not give rise to any fiduciary or equitable duties on our part. We will not be soliciting any action based on Trading Ideas and it is your responsibility to seek appropriate advice.

Any opinions that we express when we discuss Trading Ideas with you will be our present opinions only and we will not have any obligation to update you in the event of a change of circumstances or a change of our opinions. We prepare Trading Ideas based upon information that we believe to be reliable but we make no representation or warranty that such information is accurate, complete or up to date and accept no liability, other than for fraudulent misrepresentation, if it is not.

If you have any concerns about any of these matters, please do not hesitate to contact us.

Kind Regards,

Jane Lattin
Assistant to Thomas Mazarakis, Head of Fundamental Strategies

2. Securities and Exchange Commission Litigation Release No. 21489, 16 April 2010 *Securities and Exchange Commission* v. *Goldman, Sachs & Co. and Fabrice Tourre,* 10 Civ. 3229 (BJ).

3. Louise Story and Gretchen Morgenson, "U.S. Accuses Goldman Sachs of Fraud," *New York Times,* 16 April 2010.

Chapter 3

Betting with the House

Better Than Forecast

These three simple words have unbelievable power to influence financial markets: "Better than forecast." Most calendar weeks are crowded with significant financial news; each announcement is preceded by a flurry of forecasts and predictions. Financial instruments often react violently to the differences between an announced economic metric and its consensus estimate. Examples include the Consumer Price Index (CPI), Producer Price Index (PPI), Jobless Claims, Housing Starts, New Home Sales, Balance of Trade, Durable Goods Orders, Consumer Sentiment Indexes, and a variety of metrics regarding manufacturing, productivity, and spending—the list is long enough to guarantee a few significant events each week.

Most investors don't understand that the market moves from announcement to announcement and that these numbers are the principal driving forces underneath the behavior of their investments. Consumer sentiment comes in weaker than expected, the trade deficit shrinks, and consumer prices fall slightly—all are signs that consumer spending is trailing off. Stock prices for consumer products companies suddenly fall, triggering a drop in the Dow. But the dollar also weakens and foreign money flows back into the U.S. equity markets. The push-and-pull of a weaker dollar versus negative financial news takes hold, and the market eventually finds an equilibrium point. Stock prices fall, then rise, then fall again until the news has been fully digested. Bonds and currencies are also affected. Eventually, the different markets all find balance points and begin waiting for the next announcement.

Nobody understands these dynamics better than politicians, and nobody is in a better position to manipulate the numbers since most are published by the government. The length and complexity of most economic reports create endless opportunities for manipulation. One of the best-known examples appears in the Bureau of Labor Statistics (BLS) monthly Employment Situation Report.

The full report, typically 40 pages or more in length, includes detailed information broken out by gender, age, industry, and many other parameters related to type and length of employment. All of this information, however, is normally reported as a single aggregate number of jobs created or lost across the entire economy. At best, the reported number is an oversimplification. Unfortunately, it is also adjusted to account for the net employment change caused by the formation of new businesses and the loss of existing ones. This adjustment, known as the birth/death model, has become highly controversial because it is both large and impossible to verify. According to the BLS, the adjustment comes from an econometric model that forecasts the net impact of business births and deaths.[1] Simply stated, the BLS uses modeling rather than actual sampling because there is no way to immediately count the appearance of a new business.

This methodology often leads to surprisingly large corrections that cast into doubt the validity of the report. Discrepancies can be staggering. In May 2009, for example, the adjustment added 220,000 jobs, reducing the overall loss to 345,000. Left uncorrected, the loss would have been a staggering 565,000 jobs. That said, analysts had originally forecast the loss of 520,000 jobs. The birth/death adjustment turned a large forecast loss into a surprise improvement over the previous six months.

Virtually any statistician or scientist would frown on a methodology that yields a value of 345,000 with a built-in 220,000 correction designed to compensate for inaccuracies in the initial measurement. Critics who follow the reports have elaborated extensively on its shortcomings. Most of the criticism is focused on the inaccuracy of the measurement during a recession. Suppose, for example, that a small construction company goes out of business and fires 100 employees. The birth/death model assumes that a certain percentage of these employees will launch new companies, adding a large number of jobs to the economy. That assumption is incorrect, and the magnitude of the error varies with the strength of the economy. It becomes wildly incorrect during a steep recession.

To partially compensate for inaccuracies in the model, the BLS "re-anchors" its results once a year with a second adjustment known as a "benchmark." The benchmark replaces sample-based employment estimates with full population counts available through unemployment tax records filed by employers. Final adjustments based on first-quarter unemployment data are released in various forms beginning in October. Although the exact timing for partial release of this information varies from year to year, the complete report is scheduled for release in February along with the January Employment Situation Report. Once the complete benchmark report is available, corrections are applied to all months beginning with April of the previous year. A new table containing the modified numbers for April through December of the previous year suddenly appears on the BLS Web site alongside the original version. Birth/death adjustments for January, February, March, and all future months are calculated using these corrections until the next benchmark becomes available.

Table 3.1 contains preliminary and benchmark-corrected birth/death adjustments for April through December 2009. The calculations were published on the BLS Web site after the March 2009 benchmark became available in February 2010. According to the BLS, the cumulative net birth/death model added 585,000 jobs, compared with a much larger estimate of 990,000 that appeared in the originally published monthly reports that were based on the previous year's benchmark.[2]

TABLE 3.1 *Preliminary and Benchmark-Corrected Birth/Death Adjustments for April Through December 2009 (All numbers in thousands)*

Month	Preliminary	Corrected
Apr	226	126
May	220	186
Jun	185	133
Jul	32	–10
Aug	118	98
Sep	34	0
Oct	86	50
Nov	30	–23
Dec	59	25
Total	**990**	**585**

Although large, differences between original and benchmark-corrected estimates are often smaller than differences between corrected and final actual values. For example, the final corrected analysis covering the 12 months ending in March 2009 revealed that a 711,000 job gain thought to have occurred during the previous 12 months was actually a 68,000 job loss—a swing of 779,000 jobs to the downside. The original monthly numbers that predated the March benchmark correction contained an even larger adjustment of 895,000 jobs—963,000 more than the final calculation.

Confusing as this process might seem, it has been oversimplified for this discussion. The actual calendar includes a series of preliminary, corrected, and final monthly numbers, in addition to quarterly and weekly reports.

Numbers are also reported both as seasonally adjusted and not seasonally adjusted. The seasonal adjustment is particularly distressing to investors and market analysts trying to make sense of the reports because it has a history of creating tremendous swings in the results. Table 3.2 illustrates the magnitude of the swings with a listing of initial (1st), corrected (2nd), and final (3rd) seasonally adjusted month-over-month employment change numbers. Non–seasonally adjusted numbers appear in the rightmost column. April through December 2009 was chosen as a complement to Table 3.1.

TABLE 3.2 *Seasonally and Non–Seasonally Adjusted Month-over-Month Non–Farm Employment Numbers for April Through December 2009 (Initial [1st], corrected [2nd], and final [3rd] values appear in columns 2–4; final non–seasonally adjusted numbers are listed in column 5. Results are tabulated using the March 2009 benchmark.)*

		Seasonally Adjusted		Non–Seasonally Adjusted
2009	1st	2nd	3rd	Final
Apr	-539	-504	-519	214
May	-345	-322	-303	300
Jun	-467	-443	-463	-164
Jul	-247	-276	-304	-1,554
Aug	-216	-201	-154	-100
Sep	-263	-219	-139	372
Oct	-190	-111	-127	646
Nov	-11	4	64	80
Dec	-85	-150	-109	-521

Seasonally adjusted numbers are the focus of each monthly report, and the numbers reported in the financial news are always seasonally adjusted. The correction is designed to remove regularly occurring fluctuations due to predictable events such as the beginning and end of the school year, major holidays, and seasonal weather changes. If not removed, these fluctuations can obscure underlying employment trends, especially when they are significantly larger than the change being measured. For example, employment in education declines by about 20% at the end of the spring term and later rises with the start of the fall term. This seasonal change is large enough to swamp out the emergence of virtually any new trend in the industry. In theory, subtracting the known fluctuation allows minor changes to be discerned. The overall seasonal adjustment is the sum of many individual corrections. Unfortunately, as revealed in Table 3.2 the adjustment tends to be much larger than the number being reported.

Despite the confusion and acknowledged inaccuracies, reported results often generate large moves in the market, creating and erasing hundreds of billions of dollars of value. Sometimes the market rises sharply following a positive number and declines just as sharply when the corrected number is ultimately announced. The market also reacts to details regarding specific industries. A weak report can trigger a rally if a specific industry outperforms expectation.

Understanding the details underneath the monthly Employment Situation Report is important for any investor in any financial market. Details matter because the market rapidly interprets the data and sometimes reacts in surprising ways. Seemingly strong reports can be followed by a decline, weak numbers can trigger a rally, and a large surprise can result in virtually no change at all. Increases and decreases in specific sectors can differentially affect the dollar, and, as we have seen, the strength of the dollar can have profound effects on the stock market.

In summary it is fair to say that the employment reports are both misleading and confusing. Their length, complexity, and inaccuracy do a great disservice to the financial markets. Bullish investors and the government can always put a positive spin on the information, and bearish investors can usually find something negative. Worst off are the truth seekers trying to gain a balanced and accurate view because the information they seek is either missing or buried in many layers of complexity. Many believe that the information is intentionally presented in a confusing way. Others believe that the confusion is unavoidable—a natural result of the size and complexity of the economy.

Intentionally Misleading

Are the government's numbers intentionally misleading? Sometimes the answer to this question is clear; sometimes there is little doubt that the numbers have been adjusted to mislead the markets. Sharp investors who pay attention to the details can often find the footprints left by these efforts. An excellent example appears in the January 2010 Consumer Price Index (CPI) report released a few weeks later, on February 19.

Although the CPI is ultimately reported as a single number, the underlying report contains enormous amounts of data about different categories of consumer expenditure. Major categories include food, housing, transportation, clothing, medical care, education, and recreation. Each is subdivided to provide finer levels of detail about specific areas. Every line item in the report has a weighting factor that describes its overall contribution to the final answer, which, in turn, is meant to represent the overall level of inflation felt by consumers. It is customary for the BLS to report two CPI numbers—one that contains all categories and a second that excludes food and energy, which tend to be more volatile than the others.

The January 2010 results were especially meaningful because consumer prices rose less than expected, while prices excluding food and energy actually fell, something that had not occurred in more than a quarter-century. It was great news. But there was one problem—the numbers were wrong!

Housing is the most heavily weighted factor in the report. In January 2010, it represented 42% of the total CPI. Underneath this important category are three subcategories: Shelter, Utilities, and Furnishings and Operations. Shelter is the largest of the group, with a total weighting of 32%—that is, the cost of Shelter is weighted as 32% of the total CPI. Table 3.3 breaks down the reported values for this important category in the January 2010 report. The shaded area, Shelter, contains misreported numbers that simply cannot be rationalized.

TABLE 3.3 *Reported Inflation Values for Housing from the January 2010 CPI Report. (The shaded area highlights Shelter—the largest contributor to the category.)*

Item and Group	Relative Importance	Seasonally Adjusted Percent Change from Dec to Jan
Housing	41.960	–0.3
Shelter	32.289	–0.5
Rent of primary residence	5.966	0.0
Lodging away from home	0.769	–2.1
Owners' equivalent rent of residences	25.206	–0.1
Tenants' and household insurance	0.347	0.4
Fuels and utilities	5.081	0.5
Household furnishings and operations	4.590	–0.1

The calculation is simple. All we have to do is multiply the weighting for each of the subcategories by its seasonally adjusted change, add up the results, and divide by the weighting for the whole category. The final answer should exactly equal the 0.5% decrease reported for the cost of Shelter:

$$(5.966 \times 0) + (.769 \times -2.1) + (25.206 \times -0.1) + (.347 \times 0.4) / 32.289 = -0.12\%$$

The report rounds to one decimal place, so the result for the category should be reported as –0.1, which is five times more than the –0.5 value listed in the table. The difference is huge because Shelter accounts for 32% of the entire CPI. We can determine the broader impact by recalculating the overall Housing result with the corrected number. The new Shelter calculation is highlighted; Fuels and Utilities and Household Furnishings remain as originally published:

(32.289 × –0.1) + (5.081 × 0.5) + (4.590 × –0.1) / 41.960 = –0.027

So the real change in the cost of housing, which accounts for 42% of the total CPI, should have been 0.0% instead of the reported –0.3%. Altering the CPI had a huge impact on the market. The S&P 500 futures spiked up roughly 0.5% the moment the data was released.

It is essentially impossible that this mistake could have been an error because the numbers are computed automatically. The program is precise. All of the other calculations, spanning 102 pages of detailed tables, cross-checked and added up correctly. Dozens of numbers that comprise the Relative Importance column added up to 100%, with three decimal place accuracy. The most likely answer is that the reported value was intentionally falsified, and the responsible individuals were simply too clumsy to fix the underlying numbers so that the final totals would exactly add up.

The fact that the government intentionally published misleading data is distressing. Worse still is the realization that other numbers in the report may also have been manipulated without the revealing mistake that made it possible to spot the altered Housing result.

Bet with the House

The fake numbers came at a critical time when economists were struggling to understand how the government could infuse $3 trillion of "stimulus money" into the economy and hold interest rates near 0% without creating runaway inflation. This view exacerbated other fears that grew out of a persistent lack of top-line revenue growth from several large corporations, rising unemployment, and a prolonged rally that had already built in at least three years of strong earnings and growth. The stock market responded to these and other risks with a sharp decline that drove the S&P 500 down 8% between January 19 and February 8. Assurances from the Federal Reserve that interest rates would remain low "for an extended period of time" were beginning to lose their impact, and the recovery rally that began in March 2009 seemed like it might be over. Shrinking consumer prices were the perfect vehicle to reinforce the Fed's low interest rate message. As we saw previously, this message translates into a weak dollar, and a weak dollar supports stock prices. A complete lack of inflation provided credibility to the Federal Reserve's promise to keep interest rates near 0%.

The market responded with a renewed rally that sent the S&P 500 up 6% over the next month. The message is simple: When the government takes aggressive action to prop up the markets, bet with the government. Many bearish investors missed this not-so-subtle point. They did their own analysis and came to the conclusion that the rally was over. Market volatility was rising, and several strong earnings reports had been met with an immediate decline of the stock price. Bears who shorted the market were wrong because they were betting against the U.S. government. They had missed one of the most important indicators, in the form of the government's commitment to take virtually any action necessary to prop up the market. Smart investors who spotted this and other suspicious financial numbers bet with the government. It's a good strategy because they have massive amounts of money, a powerful public relations machine, and control over all the most important financial reports.

This phenomenon has come sharply into focus with the appearance of the now famous "mystery buyer" who aggressively buys massive volumes of S&P 500 futures contracts, continually taking out the asking price. This trader, whoever he may be, has nearly unlimited funds and seems to step in at key times to stop potential meltdowns. Several articles about the mystery buyer have appeared on the Web, and the phenomenon has been discussed publicly by the financial news media. Many investors use this activity as a second signal. They chart the S&P 500 futures looking for high-volume trades continually executing at or above the asking price. This behavior is especially suspicious because most buyers—even very aggressive ones—will place their trades between the bid and ask.[3]

A devious mechanism has been suggested for these transactions. The logistics involve large institutional dealers buying up stock futures and selling them to the Federal Reserve at the inflated closing price. They would earn interest on these assets under the repurchase provision of the TARP program, which allows dealers to use stocks as collateral for overnight loans from the Federal Reserve. Reversing the transaction ultimately allows the dealer to book riskless profit in addition to the interest. Trading patterns of the largest dealers are suspicious because, for quite some time, they rarely lost money. Some had nearly perfect buy and sell records that were as likely as finding a needle in a haystack.

Unfortunately, nobody knows for sure because the public is not allowed to see the Fed's balance sheet. The suspicious behavior continues—and so do the editorials and articles.

Endnotes

1. Bureau of Labor Statistics Employment Situation Report, 5 March 2010, USDL-10-0256. www.bls.gov.
2. Benchmark Article, "BLS Establishment Estimates Revised to Incorporate March 2009 Benchmarks." www.bls.gov/web/cesbmart.htm.
3. See http://seekingalpha.com/article/172609-who-is-the-mystery-buyer.

Chapter 4

Identifying Trends

Highly Efficient Markets

Today's markets are fundamentally different from those of just a few years ago. One of the most important changes has been the explosive growth in algorithmic trading that has been driven by the availability of cost-effective supercomputing and very high-speed communication links between systems. Brokers and large hedge funds exploit these advances to gain an advantage in the marketplace that is not available to the average investor.

Private investors almost always underestimate the impact of the growing gap between their capabilities and those of large institutions. The misconception is destructive when it causes them to rely on technical charting methods that might have worked well as recently as 2007 but are completely useless today. In this regard, high levels of market efficiency are the enemy.

Suppose, for example, you discovered that a particular stock tended to reverse direction when the 23-day moving average crossed the 74-day moving average. Let's also assume that the prediction works 55% of the time. If these observations were reliable, they would represent an advantage that could be leveraged into an enormously profitable trading strategy. Unfortunately, this scenario also assumes that thousands of other investors with automated pattern search algorithms have been unable to discover the same distortion. It also assumes that institutional traders armed with supercomputers and teams of "quants" were unable to make the same discovery—because if they had, their trading activities would already have erased the opportunity.

In this context, it is also important to refine the meaning of the phrase "make the same discovery." If the prediction is reliable, then it will also be accompanied by other detectable changes. At the time of the moving average cross, for example, the volume might spike or the bid-ask spread might widen. Option volumes and option bid-ask spreads might also react, the put/call ratio might shift, or single stock futures might move slightly ahead of the cross. Other technical indicators might also display changes that occur just ahead of the moving average cross. The market will quickly discover every single one of these disturbances—no matter how subtle—and the inefficiency will be extinguished.

Whereas private investors tend to overrate the value of their discoveries, large investment houses are able to identify and exploit market inefficiencies in very brief time frames. In many cases, they have large servers connected directly to the exchange processing data in real time and trading in and out of positions before private investors can even detect the changes. These systems are able to consolidate and analyze data from several different markets and place trades in the time span of a single tick. The price changes visible to private investors result from the combined activities of hundreds of computer programs all trading against each other. Large institutional traders have even resorted to creating programs that are designed to trick other programs into taking positions. A private investor with an internet-connected computer, trading platform, and technical analysis software is no match for these systems.

Algorithmic trading has also advanced, in the sense that it is built on very complex indicators that span many different markets to discover real but short-lived inefficiencies. For example, a program might decide to take a long position on S&P 500 futures because, for a brief instant, a predefined mixture of ratios between the price changes of gold, bonds, the S&P 500, and a basket of currencies seemed to be slightly distorted. The computer might use a complex weighting function to measure and compare the changes; the position might be opened and closed in just a few seconds. If many computer programs were tuned to detect the same changes there might be a surprisingly large price change as they all opened long positions. The upward price change might be followed by a rapid reversal when the trades are closed. Sometimes a series of such events results in what appears to be a trend. These events, visible to the private investor, tend to give the impression of predictability. In this regard, it is easy to be fooled by randomness.

Sadly, an entire industry has grown up around the concept that the recent price history of a stock somehow encodes information about its future. There are websites, software, consulting services, classes, and hundreds of books all devoted to teaching investors how they can predict the direction of a stock. Each year hundreds of millions of dollars are spent on these products by ambitious private investors seeking the Holy Grail. The financial media supports this misconception by highlighting chart features such as moving average crosses, stochastics, relative strength, momentum, volatility surges, price channels, and support/resistance levels. But if the people presenting this information could really predict the direction of a stock, they would be sitting at home making fistfuls of money with absolutely no interest in telling anyone how they accomplish that feat. But they can't, and that's why they are willing to hype and/or sell their expertise for relatively small amounts of money.

The Technical Charting Fallacy

Stocks react to news. This simple statement has broad implications and far-reaching conclusions that are not immediately apparent. Prices remain mostly unchanged, drifting up and down slightly, when the available news is relatively unimportant. During these calm periods, the lack of high-impact news that can be directly linked to individual companies causes investors to focus their attention on rumors, politics, editorials, and small trends that seem to emerge in the broad financial universe. They gravitate to new pieces of information and interpret every story as if it somehow impacts their investments.

The lack of significant news causes individual stocks to drift up and down in relatively narrow price ranges.

The small changes visible on a stock chart are driven by investors' desire to find hints in whatever news they can find and to overinterpret relatively meaningless pieces of information. These dynamics continue until the first piece of high-impact news appears. Affected stocks immediately jump to new prices that are set by the combined activities of thousands—sometimes millions—of traders. These activities are the underlying fuel for the price discovery engine that constantly determines market prices. During calm periods, the engine runs at idle, with stocks drifting up and down aimlessly. Adding news is like adding fuel and turning the throttle. The engine runs faster as traders enter the market and volume increases. Prices change rapidly until the fuel—in this case, the news—runs out.

The chart patterns that have become so important to millions of traders are a direct result of these dynamics. Unfortunately, the investment world has come to believe that the patterns they see in their charts somehow drive the market. But sometimes the news contradicts the chart pattern and the stock moves sharply in a direction that could not have been predicted using any calculation or mathematical transformation of the chart. Technical chartists respond to these situations by declaring that the stock has "broken out" of its range. During calm periods when price changes gradually settle into a narrow range, continuously decreasing highs and lows tend to form shapes on the chart that resemble a triangle. This shape, often referred to as a "flag pattern," appears on charts composed of vertical bars that define the high and low for each time frame being measured—minute, half hour, hour, day, etc. The bars become progressively smaller as a result of lower highs and higher lows. When a market-changing piece of news finally arrives, the resulting sharp move of the stock terminates the pattern. Market technicians interpret this move as a "breakout" that they believe to be a necessary result of the pattern.

This view is flawed because, in the absence of important news, the stock will continue to drift and the flag pattern will eventually dissolve into history. Market technicians seem to always find patterns in the drifting. They often talk about "stochastics"—parameters that vary randomly within a fixed range. In response to these dynamics, they draw lines on the chart that define a "price channel." The lines bracket the upper and lower ends of the perceived range, causing the channel to rise and fall with the stock price. Various calculations are used to define the space between the lines. Some are related to averages of the highs and lows; others use statistical measures such as the standard deviation of the prices. In all cases, the space between the lines tends to narrow as time progresses because the stock, in the absence of news, remains calm. Once a piece of news arrives and the stock begins to move, it "breaks out" of the range by crossing one of the lines. Market technicians interpret the price spike as a result of the narrow space between the lines they drew when the stock was quiet. They apply all sorts of analysis to the size of the move and focus on whether the stock returns to the space between the lines or continues in a new direction. This view and its associated technical analysis ignores the true underlying cause of the price change. It assumes that the stock was somehow gathering steam and preparing for a large price change. This process, often referred to as "consolidation," is sometimes described in surprisingly human terms by the financial news media. The commentary often describes the stock as "resting" and the market as being "tired." Sometimes these descriptions are extended with technical analysis that attempts to predict the magnitude and direction of the next price change. Large price changes are thought to follow long periods of "rest." Unfortunately, the chartists don't understand that for this analysis to work it would need to predict the importance of the next piece of news.

Although popular, none of these approaches have ever been shown to be statistically valid. Financial markets are simply too efficient. The combined insights of millions of traders built on an endless stream of instantly available news, coupled with supercomputers that trade in the millisecond time frame, remove any possible advantage that can be gained from looking at a chart. Investors should, therefore, assume that the price of a stock constantly reflects every relevant piece of information and that the next price change will reflect the impact of the next piece of news.

Decorating the Chart

The financial world is a zero sum game in the sense that every penny of profit captured by one investor must be lost by another. Technical charting strategies are among the most difficult to pursue because they pit the private investor, armed with an internet connection, desktop computer, and off-the-shelf software, against large institutions with nearly limitless computer power and direct access to real-time data. Institutional traders are able to consistently win that game and take money out of the market and, more specifically, the brokerage accounts of private investors.

Recognizing this limitation is difficult because it requires abandoning the view that you can discover a unique set of indicators and conditions that will consistently deliver large profits. It's a humbling realization that most investors would rather not accept. But recognizing this limitation is an excellent first step that begins the process of discovering better approaches in which the private investor is not disadvantaged against large institutions.

The advantage enjoyed by institutional traders is greatest in the immediate time frame. It's a speed advantage that depends on analyzing large amounts of information very quickly and recognizing trading patterns faster than other investors. Capitalizing on this advantage requires leaping ahead and placing trades that benefit from what is about to happen. The trades are usually closed about the time they begin to make an impression on the charts of private investors. But over long periods of time, stocks display complex but predictable behavior that is driven by the broad economy and a variety of market dynamics. Smart private investors who do their homework and follow the financial markets can run with the best institutional investors over long periods of time.

The simplest and best approach combines two important sources of information that everyone has access to—the daily stock chart and readily available financial news. Separately, they're not all that useful, but the combination is much more valuable than the sum of the individual parts. Step one is to decorate the chart with news items. Figure 4.1 shows daily prices for U.S. Steel and associated news items. The illustration spans approximately eight months, beginning in September 2009 and ending in late April 2010. Numbers on the chart mark news items that are listed after the figure.

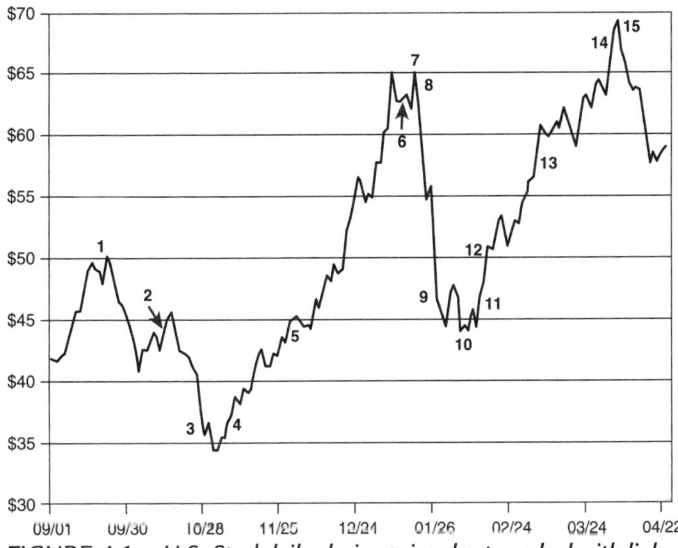

FIGURE 4.1 *U.S. Steel daily closing price chart marked with links to relevant news items (see text for headlines and descriptions).*

Each of the following items consists of a sentence or two extracted from the news article; in some cases the headline alone is used.

1. Citigroup analyst forecasts slumping metal demand due to rising stockpile of unsold vehicles.

Global steel output rises in August, according to the World Steel Organization. China remains the major growth engine for demand.

2. Steel demand likely to spike in 2010 despite previous forecasts according to the World Steel organization.

3. U.S. Steel Swings to $300 Million Loss But Forecasts Higher Demand

   U.S. Steel Beats Consensus Estimates—$2.11 loss was 77 cents ahead of analysts' forecasts. Revenue also exceeded expectations and several idle factories were reactivated.

   Citigroup upgrades AK Steel to buy—reiterates buy rating on U.S. Steel.

   Weak dollar, GDP report spark commodities rally.

4. U.S. manufacturing sector grew in Oct—Institute for Supply Management (ISM) report.

   Factory orders rise 0.9 percent in September.

   Dollar declines as Fed holds interest rates low.

   Toyota surprises with profit, boosts forecast.

5. Goldman Sachs forecasts recovery in steel due to strong demand.

   ISM survey reports that steel outlook has improved.

6. Alcoa Aluminum reports disappointing earnings.

7. U.S. Steel upgraded by Deutsche Bank.

8. Stocks fall on weak bank earnings and reports of new lending restrictions in China.

China's economy soars 11 percent in the 4th quarter setting the stage for policy tightening.

9. U.S. Steel reports a net loss of $267 million for the 4th quarter, down from a profit of $290 million for the same quarter in 2008. Sales are hurt by soft demand. Results are 30 cents per share worse than analysts' expectations.

   Fitch Ratings downgrades U.S. Steel to junk bond status.

   December durable goods orders rise slightly—0.3%.

10. Jumps in manufacturing activity and consumer spending lift stock prices; Dow gains 118 points.

    European steel output forecast to grow 0.6% in 2010 and 4% in 2011 by Eurofer Trade Group. Consumption fell 35% in 2009.

    Factory orders post large (1%) increase in December, led by gains in demand for metals and machinery.

11. U.S. trade deficit surges to $40.18 billion in December, much larger than expected.

12. Reports on industrial production and home construction boost hopes for sustained recovery.

    Leading indicators rise 0.3 percent in January for 10th straight gain.

13. U.S. Steel upgraded by Argus.

14. Construction spending falls to lowest level in 8 years—recovery threatened.

15. Minutes from the most recent Federal Reserve meeting reveal that policymakers are worried that the economic recovery may lose steam going forward, despite recent moderate improvements.

Consumer borrowing declines in February, reflecting weakness in credit cards and auto loans.

Reading through the list helps clarify the underlying forces responsible for the sharp rallies and declines evident in the chart. U.S. Steel was chosen for this example because it displayed strong up-and-down trends. But can we rationalize the trends and reversals against the news? Yes.

The first downdraft began in mid-September with two different analyst reports (1). The first reported that demand was beginning to slump; the second forecast that global steel output was rising. China had become both the largest consumer and producer. These dynamics created a complex picture in which the profitability of U.S. Steel became intricately linked to construction, manufacturing, and steel production in China. The market dislikes uncertainty, and that's exactly what these complex dynamics created. As a result, the stock began selling off.

The stock continued drifting down until a few weeks later, in late October, when new information began to reverse the direction. The first piece of news came on October 12, when the World Steel organization published a report revealing that steel demand was likely to spike in 2010 (2). The report specifically reversed previous forecasts, and the stock began to rally. However, conflicting information always results in confusion, and the new report was not sufficient to completely tip the scales in the forward direction. Moreover, the report was about the steel industry and not specifically U.S. Steel, so the effect was limited. Then during the final week of October, a series of specific news items sharply reversed the downward trend (3).

The first item was a quarterly earnings report that revealed a $300 million loss accompanied by a higher demand forecast. The news was strongly positive because the loss was significantly smaller than previous forecasts. Original consensus estimates were for a $2.88 per share loss, and the actual result came in 77 cents better. But the real news in the report was that the company had reopened several idle factories because they were receiving more orders. As in all aspects of life, actions speak louder than words. No forecast or analyst report can weigh more heavily than the company's decision to reopen factories. The positive information was accompanied by a buy rating from Citigroup. Finally, on October 29, the combination of a stronger-than-expected GDP report and a weak dollar sparked a sharp commodities rally. The stage was now set for a prolonged rally of the stock.

The late October events were followed by several weeks of supporting financial news. During the first week of November, the Institute for Supply Management (ISM) reported strong growth in U.S. manufacturing, and the dollar declined sharply after the Federal Reserve held its benchmark interest rate at a record low near zero (4). It also pledged to keep the rate at this level for an "extended period." These actions set the stage for continued dollar weakness, which favors U.S. manufacturers by keeping down the relative cost of their products in the international market. More importantly, the pledge to hold interest rates low was a signal that the U.S. government could be counted on to help the situation. Toyota also aided the situation by surprising the market with a solid profit and a boost to its forecast. Demand for steel was rising, the dollar was weak, prices were low, and the U.S. government was helping. Long U.S. Steel was definitely a good bet, especially since the stock was reversing a previous drawdown that, in the light of new information, was overdone.

Two supporting news items arrived in early December—Goldman Sachs forecast of strong demand for steel and an ISM survey that reiterated Goldman's forecast (5). The dollar also remained weak, and a variety of manufacturers reported business improvements—all positive for the steel industry.

But nothing lasts forever. All trends must eventually end. For U.S. Steel, the end came on January 12, when Alcoa Aluminum reported worse-than-expected earnings (6). Alcoa traditionally kicks off the earnings season. Shares of the bellwether immediately fell 10%. But the real problem wasn't missing analysts forecasts; it was the CEO's mention of "demand destruction." If demand for metals was falling, then the economic recovery must be faltering and the outlook for steel must be weaker than revealed in recent reports. Worse still, this news came after U.S. Steel had rallied an unprecedented 85% in just 10 weeks. The stage was now set for a sharp correction.

The stock had a brief reprieve on January 19, when it was upgraded by Deutsche Bank. But as always, details matter. The analyst, David Martin, admitted in his report that "visibility in the supply chain remains limited" and that "most of our trade contacts remain skeptical of the recent recovery." The brief rally visible at point 7 on the chart was caused by short-term technical traders betting on the stock and "retesting" its 52 week high, visible as a peak just ahead of the Alcoa Aluminum report.

These subtleties might seem difficult to navigate, but the problem can be simplified. The real question is this: Would you buy the stock after a prolonged rally, at a 52-week high, with the metals market weakening and a major industry analyst admitting that most of his industry contacts are "skeptical of the recent recovery"? The answer is no, and the momentary spike at point 7 represented a great chance to sell or go short.

Such transitions are always complex, and they almost always occur before very sharp downward corrections. Disappointing earnings reports and uncertainty in the market at the top of a long rally triggered a sharp correction that took the S&P 500 down 8.5% between January 20 and February 8. U.S. Steel exaggerated the correction because it had experienced an enormous rally.

The final nail in the market's coffin came on January 20 when the Chinese government revealed that it was instituting lending restrictions to slow down the blistering growth of its economy (8). The situation was compounded by surprisingly weak earnings reports from Bank of America and Morgan Stanley.

The situation worsened on January 26 when U.S. Steel reported a net loss of $267 million for the 4th quarter—earnings were 30 cents per share worse than analysts' expectations (9). As always, the company's statements about its business were the most significant piece of news. They painted a negative picture of a sluggish economy with shrinking demand for steel. Although the company was losing money, they forecast improved demand and a return to profitability after the first quarter. The report was mixed; automotive and appliance order rates had stabilized at the highest levels in 12 months across Europe and North America, whereas construction demand remained weak.

This time frame contained other elements of mixed news. On January 27, Fitch Ratings downgraded the company to "junk" status, citing a lack of visibility into a return to profitability. This news was also relatively low impact because it was a direct response to factors that were already known and discussed in the earnings report. Although not a strong reason to buy the stock, the downgrade was also not a strong sell signal.

January 28 brought the first positive sign in several weeks, when the Commerce Department reported that orders for durable goods had edged up a slight 0.3% in December (9). Although significantly weaker than the 2% increase expected by many economists, the increase seemed to signal that the economy might be bottoming out. Such news often acts as a coiled spring that can propel the market forward if confirmed by more positive signs. The December increase was supported by a 3.6% jump in orders for motor vehicles and parts, the biggest one-month gain in this troubled sector since May 2007. But most important of all for this analysis, demand for steel was up 8.1%.

Stocks rocketed ahead a couple of days later, on February 1, when the Institute for Supply Management reported that its index of U.S. manufacturing activity grew for a sixth straight month to the strongest level since August 2004 (10). The ISM's manufacturing index jumped to 58.4 in January from 54.9 in December, well above the 55.5 that analysts polled by Thomson Reuters had expected. Any reading above 50 signals growth. The news drove the Dow up 118 points, and U.S. Steel jumped nearly 7%. Supporting news items surfaced over the next few days. First came a report from the Eurofer Trade Group that European steel output was rising steadily. On the same day (February 4), the Commerce Department reported that factory orders had risen 1%, double the 0.5% originally forecast by economists. It was the eighth increase in nine months. These news items certainly signaled the beginning of a turnaround.

This positive news was reinforced on February 10 when the Commerce Department reported that the December trade deficit was 10.4% higher than the November imbalance (11). The surge represented a long-hoped-for increase in spending by American consumers. It also included a 3.3% increase in exports of goods and services, reflecting strong gains in sales of commercial aircraft, industrial machinery, and U.S.-made autos and auto parts—exports were strong and spending was even stronger.

All rallies need confirmation to continue. Timing is important. Strong news every few weeks is normally enough to sustain the momentum. The rally that began at points 10 and 11 on the chart strengthened on February 17 with the Federal Reserve's report on industrial production (12). The report strengthened hopes that the economy would sustain its recovery with reported gains in all three major categories: manufacturing, mining, and utilities. It was the first such collective show of strength since August. Manufacturing output rose 1%, led by a nearly 5% gain in auto production. Home construction hit a six-month peak.

Positive as this news seemed, it was somewhat tempered the next day when a report from The Conference Board, a private research group, revealed that its index of leading economic indicators had risen just 0.3%. The small increase hinted that the pace of growth was slowing. It was markedly weaker than the 1.2% rise recorded in December and the 1.1% increase attributed to November. It was also smaller than the 0.5% gain that economists had originally forecast. Some economists voiced concerns that the economy might begin to stagnate as government support programs wound down and unemployment remained high.

Growth is growth, and U.S. Steel continued to rally as the economy showed signs of improvement. An upgrade by Argus Research on March 5 continued to fuel the rally (13). This momentum continued until April 1, when the Commerce Department reported that spending on construction projects around the country fell by 1.3% to a seasonally adjusted annual rate of $846.23 billion, the lowest level since November 2002.

This news was damaging, especially because the stock had, once again, achieved a new 12-month high (14). As before, short-term technical traders aggressively traded the stock, betting on its ability to retest and sustain a new high. As we saw in January, the stock becomes very unstable when a significant peak is accompanied by negative news.

The negative view was strengthened one week later when minutes released from the March 16 Federal Open Market Committee meeting revealed that several members were concerned that the economic recovery could not be sustained over time without a substantial pickup in job creation, which had not yet become evident in the data (15).

The final nail in the rally's coffin came the next day, on April 7, when the Federal Reserve reported that borrowing had declined by $11.5 billion in February. This number was surprisingly weaker than the $500 million gain that economists had expected. It knocked the legs out from under the rally and raised questions about future demand for steel. There was no question that the recovery was losing steam—a negative sign for steel manufacturers.

As with any heavily traded stock, the performance of U.S. Steel is somewhat tied to the behavior of the broader market. This effect is also visible on the chart. For example, the small decline that took place during the second half of October 2009 mirrored weakness in the broad market (2). During this time frame, the S&P 500 fell approximately 4.5%. This decline, however, was immediately followed by the sharp rise that spans the time frame beginning in early November 2009 and ending in mid-January 2010 (points 4–6). As before, the stock's behavior mirrored that of the market, which climbed 11% with virtually no interruptions.

Predicting Reversals

Perhaps the most important part of this analysis involves predicting reversals. This example contains several significant transitions that reverse the direction of the stock and begin a new trend in the opposite direction.

Predicting the beginning of a trend is always difficult; predicting the end is usually much easier. Simply stated, a trend ends when the forces that sustain it begin to fail. This simple observation has wide-reaching implications. For example, the sharp rally visible on the chart between points 3 and 4 and points 6 and 7 was fueled by several identifiable forces, including a weak dollar, analyst upgrades, and news that factory orders were on the rise. During this time frame, U.S. Steel piggybacked on the strength of the overall market, which also climbed sharply. The rally ended abruptly in mid-January (7), when Alcoa Aluminum reported disappointing earnings. The dollar also began strengthening against the euro as credit problems began to emerge in several countries—most notably Portugal, Italy, Greece, and Spain. The drawdown was also fueled by a series of reports that revealed slower-than-expected growth in consumer spending. But the most important trigger for the reversal was news that the Chinese government was taking swift action to slow down the growth of its economy (8). Stated differently, the largest and fastest-growing steel customer was planning to reduce consumption. Such news, at the top of a significant rally, nearly always results in a correction. Forecasting the end of the November–January rally was easier than forecasting its beginning because several forces that sustained the rally seemed to be evaporating.

It is always helpful to simplify and rephrase market situations in the simplest, most direct terms. An investor who was long U.S. Steel when the news surfaced from China should simply have asked whether the stock was likely to continue to rise on negative news after it had already climbed 85% in just ten weeks. In this regard, it is important to recognize that the decision to hold a stock is exactly the same as the decision to purchase it at that price. So the question simplifies to the following:

Would I purchase the stock at this price if the following are all true?

- The stock has rallied 85% in 10 weeks.
- A related company just reported disappointing earnings.
- The largest potential market, China, has announced plans to reduce demand for the product.

Answering this simple question is certainly easier than exhaustively plowing through the company's financials hoping to find a subtle clue that you believe the market has missed. It's also far more accurate than mathematical techniques that search for clues in the recent price history of the stock—especially because none of these techniques has ever been proven reliable.

Identifying a Financial Bubble

Sometimes an uptrend seems to take on a life of its own. It grows out of control, with prices climbing exponentially over a relatively short period of time. The trend becomes a financial bubble. Unfortunately there is no simple definition of a bubble but one dynamic is clear: Bubbles grow because they become a financial black hole that attracts huge amounts of investment money. An investor who recognizes a bubble and its cause can make a lifetime of profit in a short time. Understanding the cause is critical because it will allow you to recognize the top of the bubble and exit at just the right time.

Sometimes you can leverage your knowledge of the news to identify a secondary indicator that can be used to predict the end of a financial bubble. The dramatic rise and fall in oil prices that occurred between June 2007 and December 2008 provides a perfect example. It was a wild ride for oil traders; the price skyrocketed from $68 in June 2007 to $143 in June 2008 before collapsing to less than $40 by the end of the year.

During this time frame the financial news was filled with predictions about oil. Some were based on news, others on technical indicators. Technical analysts called the top of the trend many times, and even sophisticated commodities traders lost money on wrong-way bets. Some called the top and went short at $80; others stayed long at $143. Many of the price swings were exaggerated by energy sector exchange traded funds (ETFs) that made it easy for the average investor to bet on oil prices. Energy ETFs grew in popularity until they became financial black holes, pulling in billions of dollars of investment money.

Many news items contradicted the trend along the way. For example, during the last week of November 2007, a bearish report revealed that several members of the Organization of Petroleum Exporting Countries (OPEC) had agreed to raise production in an effort to help ease high oil prices. The news was especially bearish because it came at the end of a prolonged rally, with prices approaching $100 per barrel. January futures fell more than 7%, from $95 to $88. Many traders went short believing the top had been reached. They were wrong; the rally had another 8 months and 64% to go.

Their mistake was failing to identify the forces driving the rally and understand that oil had become a financial bubble. The most important force was flexible monetary policy that flooded the U.S. economy with cash and created excessive demand for consumer products and energy. Interest rates fell steadily, and the Federal Reserve continually printed new money. Layered on top of the rising demand from U.S. consumers was the growing recognition that China was ascending to the top of the heap in terms of energy consumption. It looked as if China might soon rival the U.S. with regard to energy consumption; some analysts took bold positions and forecast $200 oil within the year.

Loose monetary policy also contributed directly to rising oil prices by weakening the dollar. This effect was most noticeable at various times when the price simultaneously fell in euros and rose in dollars. Overall, however, the price was rising because supply was struggling to keep pace with demand.

Understanding these dynamics, many traders began to chart the price of crude oil against the dollar. They followed both the financial news and the chart, looking for evidence that the dollar was strengthening. This approach made logical sense because the weak dollar seemed to be a dominant force during most of the rally. They also recognized that loose monetary policy was designed to support a fundamentally weak economy and that the limits of this approach would eventually be reached. At that point, the stimulus effect would fail, the economy would weaken, and demand would slacken off. Ironically, much of the weakness was ultimately caused by rising energy prices that became unsustainable. Rising prices eventually caused demand destruction which finally popped the bubble. These views were supported by OPEC President Chakib Khelil who, on June 26, 2008, mentioned in an interview that he attributed most of the rise in oil prices to dollar devaluation.[1] His statement wasn't exactly correct. It would have been more precise to say that the same forces that were driving down the value of the dollar were also driving up the price of oil. Dollar devaluation was more a symptom than a direct cause of the problem.

Figure 4.2 reveals the oil:dollar relationship during the 2007–2008 time frame by charting the euro/dollar ratio against the price of crude oil from June 2007 to December 2008.

FIGURE 4.2 *Euro/dollar versus Brent crude oil, June 2007 to December 2008. Brent crude prices are listed on the left y-axis (dark line), euro/dollar on the right y-axis (gray line), and dates on the x-axis. The arrow near the right side of the figure marks a significant but temporary reversal in the downtrend.*

The sharp reversal evident in the chart occurred on July 15, 2008. The Dow fell 92.65 points, posting its first close below 11,000 in two years, while oil prices retreated $6.44. Treasury prices rose and the dollar strengthened against the euro and other currencies. The next day, oil fell another $4.14 as the dollar strengthened again, and demand forecasts were lowered. The decline was strengthened by Federal Reserve Chairman Ben Bernanke's testimony to Congress concerning the weak economy. Analysts also reported that car companies were cutting back on production, airlines were slashing flights, and consumers were driving less. The Energy Information Administration also reported that U.S. crude oil supplies had risen by 3 million barrels (1%) from the previous week—the bubble was definitely bursting.

The relationship between the price of crude oil and the dollar helped predict both the top of the rally and the bottom of the decline that followed. The euro rallied sharply between February and April 2008 before becoming unstable. The price of crude oil lagged by a few weeks but continued rising until it proportionally caught up in July. Instability of the euro, visible as noise in the chart, capped the price of oil. When the euro weakened, oil fell sharply. The downtrend continued until early December, when the price of the euro again displayed significant noise. At this point, the decline in oil prices ended as the euro/dollar collapse reached its limit. These features are marked with arrows in Figure 4.3.

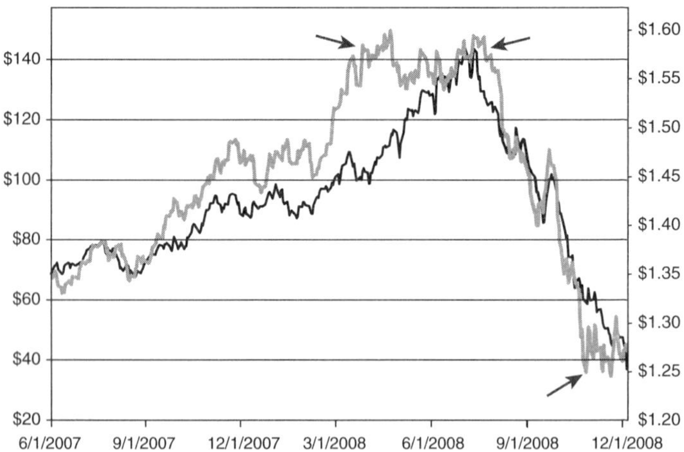

FIGURE 4.3 *Euro/dollar versus Brent crude oil, June 2007 to December 2008. Brent crude prices are listed on the left y-axis (dark line), euro/dollar on the right y-axis (gray line), and dates on the x-axis. Arrows mark areas of instability in the euro/dollar that signaled both the top of the rally and the bottom of the decline.*

Between mid-July 2008 and January 2009, investing in oil was almost exactly the same as investing in the dollar or shorting the euro. This relationship is evident on the right side of the chart as two lines that closely mirror each other. Economies were weak around the world, but the euro was far weaker than the dollar. The dynamics were complex. Rising unemployment and a weak economy in the U.S. reduced spending and demand for imported products. The U.S. had always been the consumer of last resort, and most of the world's economy depended on this demand. The slowdown caused European industrial production to fall relative to North America. This shift strengthened the dollar and weakened the euro. Two bubbles were bursting at the same time: the euro and oil. The bubbles were related because they were both built on relentless spending by American consumers who, for the most part, were spending borrowed money. Fundamental limits on the amount of money that an individual consumer can afford to borrow and spend were important contributing factors.

The following list of headlines from the financial news wires tells the story:

7/15 "Stocks End Mostly Lower as Oil Prices Retreat"

7/16 "Oil Tumbles Again; Prices Fall over $10 in 2 Days"

7/29 "Oil Hits 7-Week Low on Demand Worries, Dollar Gain"

7/31 "Oil Prices Fall Amid Weak U.S. Economic Reports"

8/4 "Oil Falls $4 After Weak U.S. Spending Report"

8/5 "Oil Below $120 a Barrel on Demand Concerns"

8/6 "Oil Prices Close Below $119 After Inventory Report"

8/8 "Stocks Jump as Oil Prices Fall Sharply"

8/11 "Oil Extends Its Slide on Signs of Demand Slowdown"

8/12 "Oil Falls Below $114 in Asia on Stronger Dollar"

8/15 "Oil Touches 3-Month Low on Stronger U.S. Dollar"

8/22 "Oil Prices Fall over $6 on Stronger Dollar"

8/26 "Oil Falls as Dollar Strengthens Against Euro, Yen"

9/2 "Oil Prices Crumble as Global Economic Outlook Dims"

9/4 "Oil Prices Close at 5-Month Low on U.S. Gas Report"

9/5 "Oil Prices Drop as Jobs Data Add to Demand Worries"

9/15 "Oil Drops $4 on Financial Turmoil"

9/16 "Oil Prices Sink Below $93 on Falling Demand"

10/2 "Oil Falls as Economy Falters"

10/10 "Oil Sinks to One-Year Low on Global Fears"

10/21 "Oil Falls Below $72 as Dollar Gains Against Euro"

11/17 "Oil Falls Below $56 as Japan Slips into Recession"

12/23 "Oil Dips Below $40 on Fears of Weaker Crude Demand"

As always, the financial news and a basic understanding of the economy were the best indicators. Many investors, however, lost money trying to predict the bottom. Their mistakes were supported by occasional positive news items. In this regard, it is always important to wait for confirmation. In a sharply falling market with unstable financial metrics, false bottoms often appear and evaporate in less than a single day. For example, the following contradictory headlines appeared at different times on August 7:

10:26 am "Oil Prices Rise After Pipeline Fire in Turkey"

1:12 pm "Stocks Turn Mixed Following Decline in Oil"

The second headline revealed that the implications of the pipeline fire in the first headline were insufficient to reverse the dominant trend. The speed of the return can, by itself, be considered an indicator. Recording and measuring such events is a valuable approach that builds on a blend of financial insight and common sense.

One of the most important tests came on September 22, 2008, when the government announced the first of many economic bailout plans. News that the government planned to infuse $700 billion into the economy sharply weakened the dollar and sent gold and oil prices soaring. Brent crude climbed from $93 to $100 per barrel. Bullish traders and many analysts immediately declared an end to the decline. They believed that the dollar would continue to weaken and that oil, priced in dollars, would resume its rally. Some forecast a return to record price levels above $145. They failed to understand the overwhelming power of demand destruction, and, more importantly, they failed to recognize that the financial problems being experienced in the U.S. were symptomatic of a broader worldwide collapse that had no possible chance of increasing the demand for energy. The decline resumed immediately, and new lows were established within a week. The event is marked with an arrow in Figure 4.2.

Exaggerations in the Financial News

Sometimes the financial news contains dangerous exaggerations. The September 22 reversal is an excellent example. The news wires reported that oil had rallied more than $16 in a single day, the largest increase ever recorded. Even more surprising was the high of the day, which took the price up more than $25. Unfortunately, the reference was to light sweet crude futures contracts for October delivery on the New York Mercantile Exchange that were expiring that afternoon. The sharp move was caused by traders scrambling to cover their positions before the contracts expired. Prices accelerated most in the final hour of trading, a common occurrence when a contract is about to go off the board. A private investor reading the news might not have realized that the numbers were distorted. Following is an excerpt from the Associated Press news release that came across the wires at 3:09 pm:

Oil spikes $25 a barrel on anxiety over US bailout
Monday September 22, 3:09 pm ET

Oil prices shoot up over $25 a barrel as anxiety over US bailout weighs on dollar

NEW YORK (AP)—Oil prices spiked more than $25 a barrel Monday—the biggest one-day price jump ever—as anxiety over the government's $700 billion bailout plan, a weak dollar and an expiring crude contract ignited a dramatic rally.

Light, sweet crude for October delivery jumped as much as $25.45 to $130 a barrel on the New York Mercantile Exchange before falling back to settle at $120.92, up $16.37. The contract expired at the end of the day, adding to the volatility as traders rushed to cover positions; the October price began accelerating sharply in the last hour of regular trading, a common occurrence when a contract is about to go off the board.

Still, the rally, which shattered crude's previous one-day price jump of $10.75, set June 6, showed the intensity of emotion in the market. The Nymex temporarily halted electronic crude oil trading after prices breached the $10 daily trading limit. Trading resumed seconds later after the daily limit was increased.

The November crude contract, which became the front-month contract at the end of Monday's session, was trading at $108.69, up $5.94, still a sharp gain.

A few key features of the story are critical to the analysis. First, it is clear that the price spike was caused by a combination of factors—the two most relevant were the announced $700 billion bailout plan and the expiration of the front-month futures contract. Second, the price spiked up $25 and then sold off to close up $16. That type of behavior rarely signals the beginning of a new rally. Third, rising oil prices cannot increase demand, and demand destruction was the dominant force driving the decline. Fourth, it is impossible to know to what extent the $7 spike in the spot price of crude oil was driven by the $16 spike in the price of the expiring contract. The fact that it significantly lagged was a strong indicator that the spike was unsustainable. Fifth, the November contract was up much less than both the expiring October contract and the spot price of crude oil. The October contract price was distorted by expiration, the spot price was driven in part by the price spike of the October contract, and the November contract (which represented a more forward-looking view) was the least affected. These large distortions are perhaps the best indicator that the price was likely to continue its decline once the futures market settled down.

Figure 4.4 reveals the oil:dollar relationship during the same time frame as in Figures 4.2 and 4.3 using NYMEX crude oil futures contracts in place of the spot price. As in Figure 4.2, the large reversal is marked with an arrow near the right side of the chart. The size of the September 22 spike is the most significant difference between the two charts. By way of direct comparison, most of the other features seem nearly identical, and it is fair to say that the overall dynamics were the same for NYMEX futures as for crude oil.

FIGURE 4.4 *Euro/dollar versus NYMEX light sweet crude front-month futures contract prices, June 2007 to December 2008. NYMEX prices are listed on the left y-axis (dark line), euro/dollar on the right y-axis (light gray line), and dates on the x-axis. The arrow near the right side of the figure marks a significant but temporary reversal in the downtrend. This feature is exaggerated by the expiration of NYMEX oil future contracts.*

Whether the September 22 rally was a temporary blip or the beginning of an uptrend is important because it was disruptive. Investors who were short oil were badly hurt by the sharp price increase; many panicked out of their positions with large losses. Others who had been sitting on the sidelines made the wrong decision and bought into what they believed was a new rally. The event has important practical implications.

Waiting for Confirmation

Although rare because of its size, the September 22 oil price spike illustrates the risk associated with investing in a market that has just changed direction. Generally speaking, it is always reasonable to expect temporary reversals and high volatility when a strongly trending market reverses and moves rapidly in the other direction. Investors who are losing money will take advantage of the reversal to reduce their losses. They typically sell aggressively at different times, depending on their view of the market and personal risk tolerance. Some investors who have lost money will attempt to hang on to their investment, hoping to recover the entire amount of the loss. As the market continues to move in the right direction, they become increasingly sensitive to the possibility of losing money that they have just recovered. This sensitivity often causes a mad rush to close positions when previously injured investors sense that the recovery might be temporary. Volatility increases along with trading volume, and the market becomes unstable.

A wise approach is to wait for the first significant retracement, which almost always follows the reversal of a powerful trend. In the case of oil, we had a sharp reversal from an uptrend to a downtrend in July 2008, followed by a retracement on September 22. The September event was short-lived, and the decline continued. As we have seen, the decline was caused by shrinking demand, which, in turn, was partly driven by high prices. The September price spike, therefore, reinforced one of the most powerful forces behind the decline. The September event was also a reflection of the weak economy, which was the underlying reason for the stimulus package. In summary, therefore, we can say that high oil prices and a weak economy caused a reversal of the uptrend. In September, during an early part of the decline, the government launched a stimulus package in an effort to help slow the collapse of the economy. The size of the package surprised the market and created financial distortions that temporarily halted the price decline. The decline resumed almost immediately, despite the enormous size of the stimulus package and the large distortions it created in the currency markets. The speed with which the decline resumed was a strong confirmation that the drawdown was likely to continue. Most bearish investors expected the decline to continue until the economy strengthened and oil prices returned to early 2007 levels.

Investors who waited for such a signal and understood both the news and the underlying price dynamics were able to capitalize on the situation by shorting oil without being injured by the September event. They were able to capture most of the downtrend by shorting oil around $100 and closing their trades below $40, for a 60% profit. During most of this time, the direction was sharply down, with only small and insignificant reversals. These dynamics highlight a simple rule that should never be broken: Never try to catch the beginning of a trend and always wait for some sort of confirmation of the new direction. Investors who break this rule by trying to sell at the absolute top or buy at the absolute bottom almost always lose because they end up being tossed around during the most volatile part of a trend—the beginning. Smart investors always wait for confirmation and they never invest if the trend can't be rationalized using the financial news and the market's behavior. Trying to time the bottom and go long is especially dangerous; it is often referred to as "catching a falling knife."

Spotting a Major Reset

Sometimes the market gives us a rare gift that comes in the form of a major change driven by a single event that is unmistakably clear and easy-to-understand. Somehow most investors miss these opportunities. In most cases, the problem is related to their inability to toss away previous information—including the chart—and recognize that everything has changed.

One of the best illustrations occurred on April 16, 2010, when the Securities and Exchange Commission (SEC) filed a civil suit against Goldman Sachs for fraud (as discussed in Chapter 2, "The Harsh Realities of the Marketplace"). It was the final day of the April options expiration cycle, a day that is normally characterized by calm behavior as many large-cap stocks trade near the strike prices that define option contracts. The news ignited a correction in financial stocks that picked up steam a few weeks later when the broad market began to decline in response to problems across Europe.

Figure 4.5 displays high, low, and closing prices for Goldman Sachs from February 2, 2010, through May 24, 2010. The April 16 event is clearly visible as a large downward spike that took the price down nearly $25 in a single day.

The large decline was simply the beginning of a continuing downward trend that continued beyond the right side of the chart. By May 24, 2010, when these words were written, the stock had fallen $50. Worse still for shareholders, the decline seemed to be accelerating. The reason was simple: The factors that precipitated the problem had not been solved. Rumors of a settlement with the SEC had come and gone, and the company seemed to be focusing a large amount of executive time on various aspects of the problem, including news media interviews, congressional testimonies, communication to customers, and legal negotiations. Superimposed on these activities were ongoing discussions among legislators about regulating the banking industry and news of criminal investigations by the Justice Department.

In such situations it is common for technical charting experts to use mathematical functions to try to predict the bottom of the decline. Much of their analysis is designed to identify "support levels" and "oversold" conditions in the chart. Others will call the bottom when they believe that the price/earnings ratio has fallen too low or that the decline in the market cap has exceeded any possible damage to the company.

Unfortunately, stocks fall through support levels all the time, and there is no reliable way to use financial metrics to predict the market's reaction to news. The simple principle that governs such situations is the market's complete lack of tolerance for uncertainty. For this reason alone, the stock price will not stabilize until all outstanding issues are resolved or the stock falls so far that even the most pessimistic speculator is willing to take a chance. In this regard, stocks that are pummeled by bad news can fall far beyond any level that makes financial sense. The Goldman Sachs case is a perfect illustration because the decline erased 27% of the market cap (approximately $27 billion) in just a few weeks, an amount equal to many times the potential cost to the company. Investors who came to this conclusion often made the mistake of buying the stock during brief reversals that occurred during the decline.

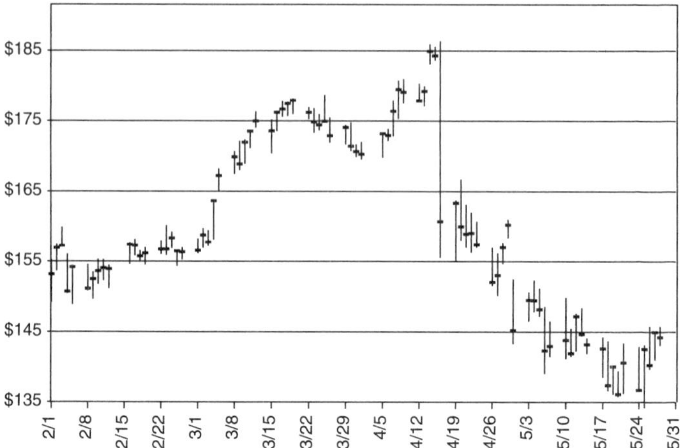

FIGURE 4.5 *High-low-close chart for Goldman Sachs, February 1, 2010 to May 31, 2010. Vertical lines mark each daily high-low; horizontal dashes mark daily closing prices. Dates appear on the x-axis.*

The collapse was also punctuated by technical analysis that revealed bottoms around $155 and $145. Many analysts believed that the April 16 event filled two gaps on the chart created during the rally. The first gap occurred in early March, when the stock spiked more than $10 in two days; the second gap occurred in early April, just ahead of the negative news. The analysis was overly complex and completely wrong.

The first true bottom was reached on May 24 when the stock touched $135. Buying behavior is evident in the large daily high-low transitions and apparent price floor that appears as noise near the right side of the chart. Sometimes technical charting makes sense, especially when it supports a financial view driven by fundamental knowledge of the company's business. In the Goldman Sachs example, it is clear that the market's price discovery mechanism had finally found a bottom and that buyers were returning. It can be assumed that the stock will remain above this floor unless additional negative news items surface that have not been factored into the price. Examples might include additional allegations of fraud or more aggressive legal behavior on the part of the U.S. government. Weak earnings, however, would be very unlikely to adversely affect the stock because the SEC-driven correction had already taken the price down to a level that was inconsistent with the company's strong business performance.

The Goldman Sachs debacle is significant because it also caused the collapse of other stocks. J.P. Morgan and Citigroup, for example, began falling when the Goldman news was announced. They continued to deteriorate as news and rumors surfaced about government investigations of other financial institutions. Figure 4.6 displays the high-low-close chart for J.P. Morgan during the same time frame as in Figure 4.5. The peak occurred on the exact same day, and the collapse was approximately the same magnitude. As in Figure 4.5, stabilization is visible near the right side of the chart.

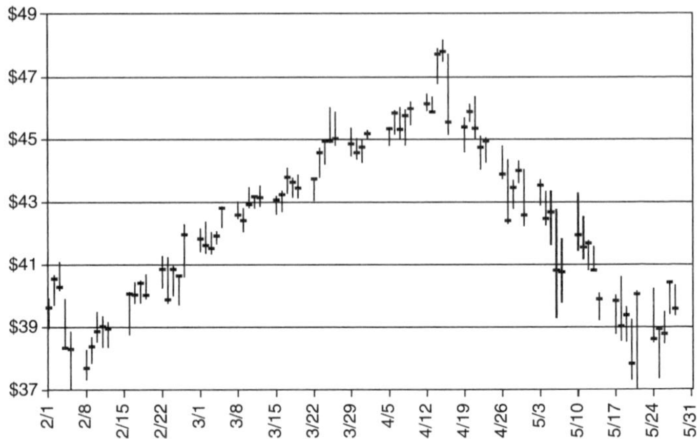

FIGURE 4.6 *High-low-close chart for J.P. Morgan, February 1, 2010 to May 31, 2010. Vertical lines mark each daily high-low; horizontal dashes mark daily closing prices. Dates appear on the x-axis.*

It is important to recognize that the collapsing prices of Figures 4.5 and 4.6 were driven by a variety of uncertainties, the most significant being the risk of extensive government regulation. Many analysts were quick to point out that even if Goldman Sachs was completely wrong and it was forced to pay penalties and interest, the amount of the damage would be insignificant. They further reasoned that the issue would likely remain in the courts for some time. This analysis is flawed because it fails to account for the market's interpretation, which includes a long list of unanswered questions and doubts. There is only so much investment money to go around, and money tends to gravitate to areas of low business uncertainty. Simply stated: A technical bottom for the stock will not occur for any simple reason that can be forecast using charts or fundamental analysis; it occurs when the market says it occurs and not before. Instead of trying to forecast the bottom, sharp investors wait for clear evidence that buyers have returned, and they wait for some confirmation of that behavior in terms of time and continued movement in the up direction. As we saw in the oil trading example, learning to wait and miss the beginning of a reversal is an important lesson.

This principle is best understood by analyzing a complete business collapse driven by financial issues whose long-term impact cannot be estimated. In the next section, we will examine two such disasters: one that has already ended in bankruptcy and another that was ongoing when these words were being written.

An Ongoing Catastrophe as a Trend

The collapse of General Motors is one of the best examples of a downward trend with no bottom. Sales began shrinking rapidly in mid-2005; by the middle of the fourth quarter, rumors surfaced that the company might eventually fail.

GM's problems were widespread and complex. Following is a brief list:

- On May 16, 2005 Standard and Poor's downgraded the company's debt to junk bond status.
- GM reported that it lost $1.6 billion in 2005's third quarter. It recorded a dismal performance in North America, where losses exceeded $4 billion for the first three quarters.

- Delphi, GM's largest parts supplier, filed for bankruptcy, and it appeared that GM, which spun Delphi into a separate company in 1999, might be responsible for up to $12 billion in payments due to GM's former employees and retirees.
- News that the SEC was investigating GM's accounting practices sent the stock tumbling 7%.
- The company revealed that it would have to restate 2001 earnings, cutting profits that year by as much as $400 million. This announcement shaved another 5% off the share price.
- Healthcare costs placed GM at a disadvantage against Asian automakers in the U.S. who had less extensive health plans, a younger workforce, and no healthcare obligations for retirees. It was clear that GM would continue to pay thousands more in healthcare costs per vehicle than Asian automakers.
- GM was facing tougher new rules on pension accounting after the Senate passed a bill that changed the status of GM's plans from fully funded to underfunded. The new rules significantly increased the company's costs. The government-backed Pension Benefit Guaranty Corp., which acts as a safety net for corporate pension plans, stated that GM's plan was underfunded by $31 billion.
- Skyrocketing gasoline prices were driving a rapid shift in sales from large SUVs and light trucks to small fuel-efficient vehicles. This news was particularly distressing because GM generated profit only from its large, gas-guzzling vehicles.

- GM's slice of the U.S. vehicle market had been declining steadily for 30 years. Its share fell from 43.8% in 1980 to 26.2% in 2005. Sales occasionally increased, but always because of costly incentives such as zero-interest financing or programs offering employee discounts to the general public. One such program was used to clear out 2005 inventory and make room for 2006 vehicles.

By November, the bankruptcy rumors had become so widespread that Chairman and Chief Executive G. Richard Wagoner Jr. decided it was time to respond. On November 16, 2005, he declared in an internal memo to his 325,000 employees that bankruptcy was "unnecessary." "There is no plan to file for Chapter 11 protection," Wagoner said flatly, calling such action "contrary to the interests of our employees, stock- and bondholders, dealers, and our suppliers and customers."

The case was simple enough: GM had $34 billion in cash and could free up roughly $15 billion more by selling various businesses. With a burn rate of only $2 billion per quarter, the company should have been stable for several years. Furthermore, the burn rate was likely to slow as a result of recent restructuring, which was designed to eliminate nine factories and 30,000 workers over three years.

At the time of Wagoner's internal memo, the stock was trading at a 13-year low; the total value of the outstanding shares was less than the amount of cash the company had on hand. Some analysts rated the stock as a buy. Their views were supported by the simple arithmetic of cash on hand versus the burn rate and the expectation that the U.S. government would step in to prevent the collapse of a large industrial icon with hundreds of thousands of current and former employees receiving medical benefits, salaries, and pensions.

In some sense they were correct because the government ultimately did assist GM, with more than $13 billion of Troubled Asset Relief Program (TARP) funds in December 2008, followed by an additional $6 billion in April and May 2009. Unfortunately, the attempt failed and the company went bankrupt.

How can we distinguish between an unstoppable downward spiral and a sharp decline that has a technical support level, such as the Goldman Sachs example? The answer is simple. It depends on three parameters: top-line revenue growth, profitability, and debt. Risk factors that add doubt to these numbers further reduce the value of the company.

GM was shrinking, it was unprofitable, and its debt was growing. The company was also plagued by risk at all levels. For example, in December 2005, Robert Hinchliffe, an auto analyst with UBS Securities, estimated that GM would burn through $1 billion to $1.5 billion per week if its North American operations were shut down by a strike at Delphi. Such a strike was considered likely by many industry analysts.

Final earnings results for 2005 were devastating. The company reported a net loss of $8.6 billion (later restated as a $10.4 billion loss)—the worst since 1992, when the company lost $23.5 billion. GM executives were honest and blunt about the problems. Rick Wagoner was quoted as saying, "Two significant fundamental weaknesses in our North American operations were fully exposed—our huge legacy cost burden and our inability to adjust structural costs in line with falling revenue." He further described 2005 as "one of the most difficult years in GM's history."[2]

Surprisingly, however, the steep decline in GM stock did not commence for two years. These dynamics highlight an important point for bearish investors: Large multinational companies can suffer financial troubles for long periods of time before they collapse. GM was a perfect example. It owned many businesses, including its lending arm, GMAC. As stated earlier, the company had access to $49 billion, with only a $2 billion per month burn rate. It also had mechanisms for reducing the burn rate: layoffs, reduced benefits for more than 450,000 retirees, factory closings, and dozens of possible negotiating points with the United Auto Workers.

Large investors also stepped in to support the company. Most notably, Kirk Kerkorian, who owned a large stake, announced on May 5, 2005, that he would purchase 28 million more shares through his private company, Tracinda Corp. His disclosure sparked the largest one-day rally in 40 years. On September 1, Tracinda Corp. announced that it would further increase its stake with the purchase of 13.1 million shares, leaving Kerkorian with control over 53.8 million shares—nearly 10% of the total market capitalization.

Between November 2005 and November 2007, the stock climbed and fell with each labor negotiation, stock purchase, layoff, and plant closing. Overall, it outperformed the broad market, which climbed 25% during the same time frame. But business continued to decline. North American sales were down 4% in 2005, 8.7% in 2006, and 6.3% in 2007. Monthly prices for this time frame are displayed in Figure 4.7.

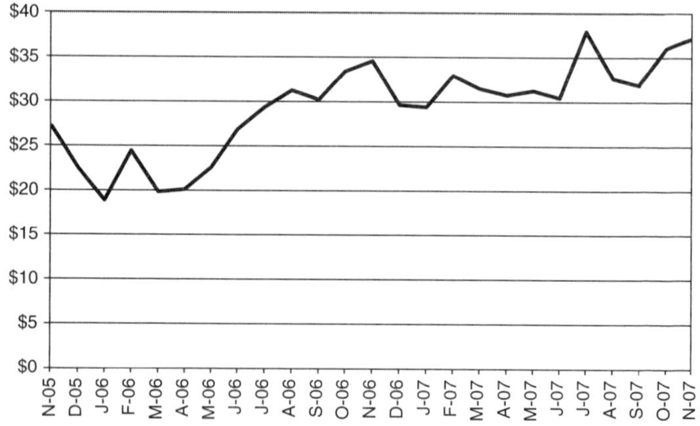

FIGURE 4.7 *General Motors monthly stock prices, November 2005 to November 2007.*

During the 2005–2007 time frame, many bearish investors lost money betting against GM. Their mistake was not waiting until GM had exhausted all its options. Financial reports were confusing during this time frame. For example, fourth-quarter 2006 earnings revealed a net income of $2.2 billion, or $3.88 per share. However, when "special items" were included, the company suffered a net loss of $2.0 billion, or $3.50 per share. "Special items" refer to unique transactions, such the sale of 51% of GMAC to Cerberus Capital Management. These numbers were an improvement over the previous year's $3.2 billion loss ($10.4 billion when special items were included).

Despite the loss, 2006 earnings were a significant improvement over 2005 earnings. The stock continued to rise and fall, with a slightly upward bias, until November 2007, when the company reported an enormous $39 billion loss for the third quarter. The loss was caused by a valuation allowance on deferred tax assets of $38.6 billion. Surprise disclosures of large losses are always a problem, regardless of the cause. In this case, the announcement triggered an immediate drop in the share price, which sent the stock down 8% to $33.25 in premarket trading. The charge was based on accounting rules that allow tax overpayments to be used as credits against future income. Credits are lost if a company doesn't earn enough to use them. Wagoner blamed "the deterioration of profitability at GMAC" for triggering the massive charge related to unclaimed tax credits. He further clarified the situation, stating, "We can, if we generate profit in the future…fully utilize the credit, so I wouldn't read anything into it as to the prospects of the company."

Overall, third-quarter results were weak and the situation was becoming more complex. Special items included the noncash charge mentioned earlier, in addition to a $3.5 billion after-tax gain on the sale of the Allison Transmission business in August 2007, for which GM received $5.4 billion. GM also had special charges of $1.6 billion in pension service costs related to prior labor agreements, $400 million associated with restructuring, and $400 million related to an adjustment to the Delphi reserve.

Excluding these special items, the company had a 2007 third-quarter adjusted net loss of $1.6 billion, or $2.80 per share. Wall Street analysts, on average, had forecast an adjusted quarterly loss of only 36 cents per share, according to Reuters Estimates.[3] The larger-than-expected loss was primarily driven by a significant decline in net income at GMAC, as well as increased corporate expense related to legacy costs, foreign exchange, and various 2006 tax benefits, partially offset by improved performance in automotive operations. Automotive revenue was $43.1 billion, with GM's share in the U.S. growing slightly (0.5%). Total corporate revenue fell to $43.8 billion, from $48.9 billion a year earlier. Most of the loss at GMAC was related to the declining housing market and associated problems in the mortgage business.

These are the kinds of confusing results that destabilize a stock. Most basically, the numbers were far below analysts' expectations since the loss was $2.80 per share, versus a consensus estimate of 36 cents. However, most of the loss occurred in the mortgage-lending business, and it could be argued that the car business was beginning to stabilize. GM had also reached a cost-cutting agreement with the United Auto Workers; as with everything else, its impact and time frame were uncertain. Overall there were too many unknowns, too many losses to explain, and not enough upside to attract investors. More importantly, the error bars associated with the calculations were becoming too large. The $38 billion one-time charge is a perfect example. If, as Rick Wagoner stated, the company generated enough profit in the future, it might be able to utilize the credit. Unfortunately, his statement only added confusion because the record one-time charge was triggered by cumulative losses over three years and the risk of both weaker auto sales and GMAC results in coming quarters—all issues that needed to be addressed as part of a turnaround strategy.

From an investor's perspective, it was virtually impossible to determine the net worth of the company and, therefore, the stock. Such situations always create a bottomless pit that stocks rarely recover from. Figure 4.8 displays monthly stock prices from October 2007 to June 2009, when the company went bankrupt. The slight peak visible near the left side of the chart was the final turning point just ahead of the 3Q 2007 earnings announcement. Over the next eight weeks, the stock fell nearly 30%.

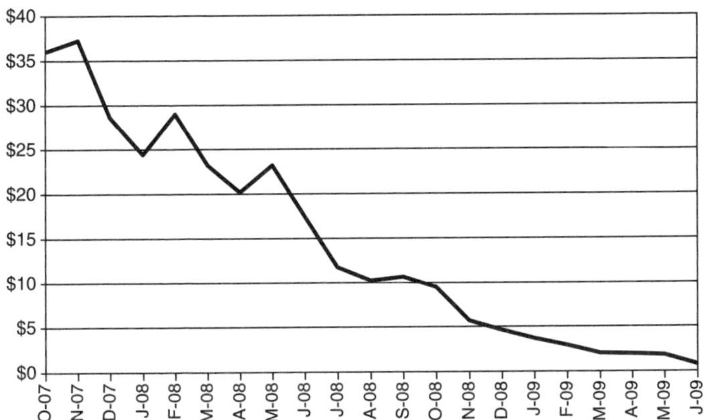

FIGURE 4.8 *General Motors stock collapse, October 2007 to June 2009.*

The collapse continued as the company attempted to shore up earnings and cut costs. For the 2008 calendar year, the adjusted net loss, excluding special items, totaled $16.8 billion ($30.9 billion with special items included). Virtually all executive attention was focused on saving the company through restructuring, layoffs, plant closings, and a variety of financial engineering exercises designed to reduce taxes and delay expenses. Revenue for the fourth quarter fell to $31 billion, from $47 billion in 4Q 2007.

A report from the auditing firm Deloitte & Touche issued on Thursday, March 4, confirmed that GM, unable to pay its bills, was standing on the brink of bankruptcy. Pointing to continuing losses—$30.9 billion for 2008 and $82 billion over the past four years—the company's negative net worth, and its inability to generate the cash needed to conduct business, the auditors said that, without billions in federal loans, there was "substantial doubt" that GM could "continue as a going concern." The auditors wrote, "There is no assurance that the global automobile market will recover or that it will not suffer a significant further downturn." Surprisingly, bullish investors who believed the government would continue to bail out the company aggressively bought stock. On June 9, after more than 100 years, General Motors filed for bankruptcy.

For the most part, investors who bought the stock during the collapse believed that their decisions were based on sound financial reasoning. Most believed that automobile sales would eventually bottom out (they were correct) and that the company had enough resources to weather the storm (they were not correct). They also counted on the U.S. government for help. Once again, they were correct because GM received a total of $19.4 billion in TARP funds between December 2008 and May 2009. Their mistake was betting on a company whose value could not be fairly determined. Although they invested in GM, they were really betting on the U.S. government's TARP program.

A striking illustration of these concepts arose during the days when this chapter was being written. The event was the famous British Petroleum (ticker: BP) oil spill in the Gulf of Mexico. It began on April 20, 2010, when an exploratory well exploded, destroying the drilling rig and killing 11 company employees. All efforts to cap the well failed, and oil poured into the Gulf of Mexico at rates generally estimated to exceed 50,000 barrels (2.1 million U.S. gallons) per day.[4] The stock decline accelerated with the recognition that the magnitude of the damage was unknown. During this disaster, BP had no friends. That dynamic became crystal clear when the President Obama publicly stated that the company would be responsible for "every penny" of the damage and cleanup.

At the time of this writing, the stock was down more than 50% from its pre-disaster price of $60.48. That decline occurred in only 46 trading days (April 20 to June 24). During this time frame, hopeful news about potential solutions generated brief rallies as large as $3. But the trend never reversed. The brief rallies were mostly related to short covering by bearish investors protecting profit. Positive news is a destabilizer for these investors, and they often close positions on the slightest hint that the stock could rise.

The most important positive event occurred on May 27 when company officials announced that they might have succeeded in sealing the well using a method known as "top kill." Most industry experts believed the probability was very small that the method would work. Furthermore, sealing the well would not have erased the billions of dollars in damage that represented the true risk to BP. Top kill failed, oil continued pouring out of the well, and the stock resumed its decline, falling $9 over the next 2 days. Figure 4.9 displays prices for BP from April 1, 2010 through June 24, 2010. An arrow marks the top kill event which failed to cap the well.

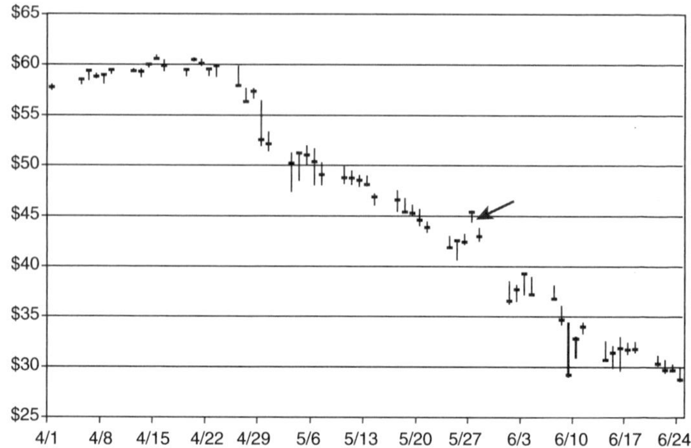

FIGURE 4.9 *High-low-close chart for British Petroleum, April 1, 2010 through June 24, 2010. The arrow near the right side of the chart marks a failed attempt to cap the well on May 27.*

These dynamics illustrate the importance of identifying the true underlying source of risk. Bullish investors looking for a bottom were badly hurt by the failed top kill attempt on May 27. But their decision to buy the stock would have ultimately been wrong anyway, because the true sources of risk were the ongoing expense of the cleanup and legal proceedings against the company. Bearish investors understood these dynamics and used the upward spike as an opportunity to short the stock. Less than two weeks later, on June 9, they had already realized a $16 profit (36%) when the stock closed at $29.20.

Learning to identify uncertainty is one of the most important skills an investor can acquire. Bullish traders learn to avoid uncertainty, and bearish investors take advantage of it. Option traders earn a living quantifying uncertainty in the form of volatility, the most important factor in the price of an option contract. Many option traders took advantage of the BP problem by selling far out-of-the-money options that were priced with extremely high levels of volatility. The simplest approach involved selling short-term call options above the original trading price of the stock before the collapse. Such trades were unaffected by brief rallies and delivered constant, steady profit. The exact same approach worked perfectly during the GM collapse. More sophisticated option traders sold long-term call options above the pre-catastrophe price and used the revenue from these option sales to purchase puts at a much lower price. They generated profit on both sides as the value of the calls they sold evaporated and the value of the puts they owned increased sharply with each decline. Such trades delivered returns in the range of 50% per week when the stock was falling sharply.

Summary

This discussion was designed to highlight the difference between a price decline driven by a specific problem that can be quantified in terms of potential damage to the company and an all-out collapse driven by an open-ended problem of unknown magnitude. Both GM and BP faced problems of unknown magnitude in which the ultimate damage to the company could not be determined. At the time of this writing, with BP stock trading in the low $30s, investors were purchasing large numbers of put options with a strike price of $2.50 and only 6 months remaining before expiration. The $5.00 strike price was even more popular and significantly more expensive. These investors were willing to risk a 100% loss by betting that the company would be bankrupt in only a few months. They were also willing to pay high prices because these contracts were priced with 170% implied volatility, more than four times the normal amount for these options. This behavior itself should be treated as a technical indicator and a sign of severe risk to anyone thinking about purchasing the stock. Activities in the option market can often be used to forecast the future behavior of stocks because option prices are based on volatility, and volatility translates into risk. We will return to a more detailed discussion of these dynamics in the next chapter.

Endnotes

1. "Oil's Rise Is Mainly Dollar's Devaluation, OPEC Chief Says," Reuters, 26 June 2008.
2. Associated Press wire, 27 January 2006.
3. "GM CEO: 'No Cash Impact' from Record Charge," Reuters, 7 November 2007.
4. Ian Macdonald, John Amos, Timothy Crone, and Steve Wereley, "The Measure of an Oil Disaster," *New York Times,* 21 May 2010. www.nytimes.com/2010/05/22/opinion/22macdonald.html.

Chapter 5

A New Era

Introduction

Over the years, investors have lost trillions of dollars because they made assumptions about the economy or, even worse, had personal opinions that were driven more by optimism than fact. The largest, most common mistake is believing that the market will return to a previous state. This flawed approach to investing is the genesis of the word "correction."

Most investors make money during a rally. When the market falls they consider the decline to be a correction, and they begin looking for signs that the correction is ending. Some are more cautious than others. They wait for, what appears to be, a significant reversal of the correction before getting back in. However, the market will only regain its upward momentum when the original causes of the drawdown have been completely addressed. Contrary to popular belief, there is no such thing as a normal correction in terms of percent.

These misconceptions are not a recent phenomenon. Most investors who lost all their money in the crash of 1929 reentered the market soon after the initial event because they believed the drawdown was a brief correction. Looking at a chart of the Dow between September 1929 and April 1930 might lead you to believe they were correct. If they had perfect timing and knowledge of the future, they would have sold everything in September, reentered the market in November, and sold again at the end of March—a nearly impossible feat.

Figure 5.1 displays the Dow from just before the crash in September 1929, to the bottom that finally occurred at the end of June 1932. Three significant false bottoms are labeled. The first and most destructive triggered a 45% rally that was large enough to fool even the most pessimistic investors. As is always the case during times of economic uncertainty, the market once again reversed direction and began falling just after everyone had been fooled into buying back in. The second false bottom was smaller because fewer investors remained to be fooled twice. By the third time, almost nobody was left standing.

Most of today's investors are well aware of the 1929 stock market crash. Many, however, don't realize that both the crash of '29 and the worldwide depression that followed marked the end of a financial bubble often referred to as the Roaring Twenties. The magnitude of the drawdown was so severe that it took more than 25 years for the market to reach its pre-crash level. In November 1954, the Dow traded at the same level as it did at its peak in September 1929. There were many different ways to make money during this time frame; staying long was not one of them.

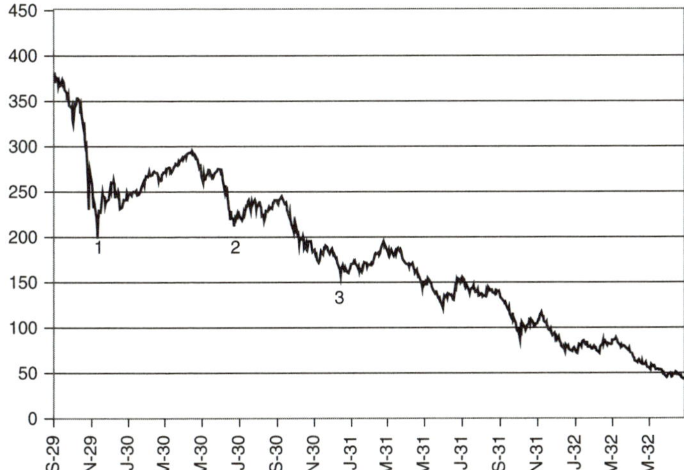

FIGURE 5.1 *The 1929 stock market crash: September 1929 to July 1932. The first three false bottoms are marked on the chart.*

Bears make the same mistakes as bulls, but in the opposite direction. They often have an opinion that the market is fundamentally weak, and they continually look for reasons to go short. This style of thinking caused the demise of many hedge funds and wealthy private investors who bet against the 5-year housing boom that finally collapsed in 2008. It was an easy mistake to make because the bubble grew to ridiculous proportions that made absolutely no financial sense. Home prices sometimes doubled in less than a single year, and banks were willing to lend money to virtually anyone without checking their credit because they accepted the home being financed as collateral. Large financial institutions compounded the risk by selling credit derivatives based on mortgage portfolios.

Bearish investors anticipating a crash shorted the housing market several times along the way because they believed they had identified the top. They underestimated both the potential size of the bubble and the U.S. government's willingness to fuel economic growth with ultra-low interest rates. Their short positions were in conflict with the government, the banks, and the vast majority of private investors. The collapse was inevitable, but the timing was impossible to predict.

Bullish investors who lost money during the 1929 crash and bears who lost money shorting the 2000s housing bubble made the same fundamental mistake as any investor who bets against a powerful trend. They failed to identify and thoroughly understand the economic forces at work. Large-scale trends that develop over long periods of time generally persist until reversed by a specific event. When the trend is a financial bubble, like the Roaring Twenties or the housing boom of the 2000s, it can grow to astronomic proportions.

This chapter makes the case that a new investment era began with the dot-com crash and NASDAQ market collapse of 2000. As we will see, because the new era is fundamentally different from those of the past, yesterday's approaches to investing are unlikely to work again for a very long time—if ever. Two characteristics dominate today's markets: leverage and instability.

The first characteristic, leverage, is a result of explosive growth in both the size and complexity of the world's financial markets. Markets that trade around the clock, instantaneous availability of news, high-frequency trading between computer systems, and the wide availability of sophisticated platforms for active traders are the underlying agents driving this complexity. The investment world has responded with a broad array of financial instruments including, at the most basic level, put and call options on stocks and indexes. Even simple positions can provide large amounts of leverage. For example, an investor who accurately forecasted General Motors' demise in 2008 could have easily generated a 20x return on a very small investment in far out-of-the-money put options. Sophisticated option traders can structure complex positions that have the capacity to return many times their cost with minimal risk.

Leverage in the form of derivatives has become a cornerstone of today's financial marketplace. Instead of simply buying or selling shares of stock, today's investors structure complex multipart positions that can be long or short puts and calls, futures, and stock. When a relatively inexpensive position delivers a tremendous return, another investor on the other side of the trade must necessarily experience an equally large loss. Sophisticated investors who structure complex positions expect these losses and normally hedge with other complex trades designed to offset or hedge their risk. Sometimes a single large hedge is structured to protect against losses in a large portfolio of trades.

During the housing boom of the late 2000s, large financial institutions with enormous portfolios of mortgages were all hedged with complex derivatives known as credit default swaps (CDS). American International Group (AIG) was, by far, the largest source of these contracts. When the housing boom collapsed, AIG was contractually required to produce $100 billion in collateral to cover its estimated $450 billion of CDS contracts. This explosion was the event that destroyed AIG. The underlying cause was leverage.

Surprisingly, nobody knows the combined size of the world's derivatives markets. Estimates vary from $500 trillion to $1 quadrillion (roughly 20x the world's GDP). Everyone should be afraid of these numbers because they represent a risk that cannot be quantified. The multiplication effect of this leverage creates enormous market swings because it magnifies the size of every loss or gain. For example, it has become common for a single investor to move around $1,000,000 in the foreign exchange markets with just $10,000 of collateral. When the market moves against that investor, his losses are magnified 100x; an entire account can be lost in just a few seconds. Other traders will say that "he was carried out." Unfortunately, the dynamics of leverage effect everyone including the most conservative investors because they create enormous market swings when a large group of highly leveraged institutional investors panic out of their positions; and that's exactly what happened when AIG collapsed.

The second characteristic, instability, is directly related to the complexity of the financial world. A major source of this complexity is the tight relationship between markets and the speed with which billions of dollars can move from one location to another. The infamous carry trade is a perfect example. Investors borrow large amounts of money at low interest rates and use the money to purchase financial instruments that deliver a safe return slightly larger than the cost of the money. If the currency strengthens, even the smallest amount, they close their trades and pay back the loans.

In today's markets carry trade transactions are completely computerized; billions of dollars can be moved in just a few seconds. The tremendous gold rally that more than tripled the price between January 2001 and January 2008 was, to a large extent, driven by the carry trade as investors borrowed yen at extremely low interest rates and used the money to buy gold. Each time the yen strengthened slightly, they sold gold and moved the money back into yen to repay their loans. The tremendous volume and speed of the transactions drove large swings in both the price of gold and the value of the yen. These changes rippled through the financial world simultaneously affecting currency, equity, and bond markets.

The next step in our discussion will be a brief historical review that creates a framework for comparing the current era to the economic boom that preceded it. As we shall see, the financial boom that began in the post World War II era continued almost uninterrupted until the NASDAQ crash more than 50 years later. This analysis sets the stage for a detailed discussion that focuses on the altered dynamics that characterize the post-dot-com era. Our analysis makes the case that technical charting has little value in the current environment. Simply stated, the discussion shows that the recent price history of a stock does not contain information that can be used to predict its future. Central to this analysis is the impact of high-frequency algorithmic trading at large financial institutions. This style of trading has become the dominant force driving the markets in the post-dot-com era. The bulk of our discussion, however, focuses on strategies and rules for investing in the complex, unstable markets of the 21st century.

Relevant History for a New Era

As we have seen, investing without understanding the underlying dynamics of the broad economy is a huge mistake. Two specific examples were previously mentioned. The first illustration involved large numbers of investors who bought into false rallies during the 1929 crash. Their mistake was trying to identify the bottom of a falling market without thoroughly understanding the dynamics that triggered the decline. Had they recognized and quantified the enormous imbalances in the world's economy, they almost certainly would have been out of the market long before October. In that regard, some of the largest fortunes in history were made by bearish investors who sat on the sidelines waiting patiently for the collapse. After the drawdown began, they shorted both individual stocks and the market. Among the most famous bears of this era was Jesse Livermore who made more than $100 million in the crash. One of Livermore's most important trading rules was to never attempt to catch the top or bottom of a trend. He understood the magnitude of the financial bubble and knew the decline would continue for some time. Figure 5.1 reveals that catching the first wave of selling was irrelevant.

In many ways, world financial markets remained unchanged from the end of World War II until the collapse of the dot-com bubble in 2000; a period of fantastic growth that lasted nearly 55 years. Packed into those 55 years were the Korean and Vietnam wars, the collapse of the Soviet Union, Japan's rise to become the world's second largest economy, the collapse of the gold standard, and the arrival of satellite communications, space travel, nuclear power, computers, biotechnology, the internet, and mobile wireless communications. Some of these events were disruptive and some represented tremendous opportunities. During this extended time frame, the one constant that investors could always count on was the resiliency of the U.S. economy. That power allowed U.S. equity markets to continue chugging along at a pace that eclipsed even the largest draw downs. Every correction from 1946 to 2000 was a buying opportunity. The constant rise is evident in Figure 5.2, which traces the Dow from January 1946 to January 2000.

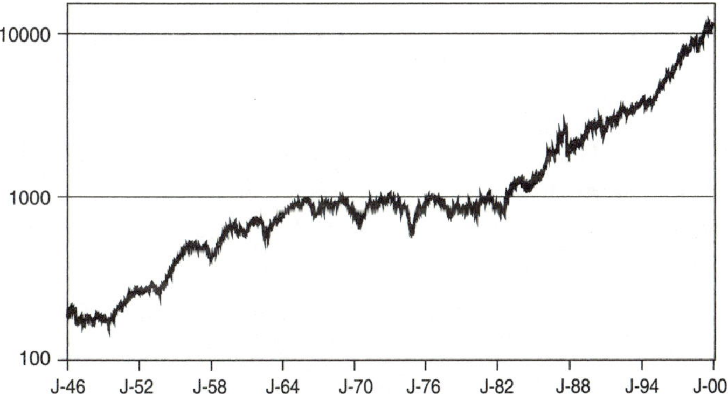

FIGURE 5.2 *Daily closing prices for the Dow Jones Industrial Average—January 1946 to January 2000. The Dow is represented on a logarithmic scale (y-axis); dates are marked on the x-axis.*

During the time frame of the chart, the rally accelerated fast enough to force the use of a logarithmic scale. A linear representation compresses the early part of the diagram hiding even the largest changes. The left half contains a fivefold increase from just under 200 to 1,000. Growth accelerates on the right side of the chart taking the Dow from 1,000 to 11,000—more than a tenfold increase over 25 years.

Using a logarithmic scale enables us to visualize two distinct periods of growth. The first begins just after the war and stalls out between 1965 and 1980 with the Dow hovering below 1,000. A second more rapid growth spurt follows. The underlying reasons can be summarized in the context of world events.

At the end of World War II, the United States was uniquely positioned as the dominant manufacturing superpower. Europe and Japan were recovering from the war, and China had yet to emerge as a powerful economic force. While the rest of the world was rebuilding, the United States was leveraging its wartime manufacturing capacity to become the world's supplier of everything from heavy machinery to electronics. Even the energy business was dominated by the United States, which had large, proven reserves of domestic oil.

These dynamics began to change in the late 1960s as other countries caught up. By 1970, Asia and Europe had established themselves as major exporters of a variety of consumer products including, most notably, electronics and automobiles. The U.S. economy entered into a transitional period that was characterized by rising inflation and diminished growth. It was during these years that the term *stagflation* became recognized as an unfavorable economic condition.

The transitional period ended in 1980, with a renewed focus on advanced technologies for computer science, medicine, and communications. Venture capital became an important economic force, Silicon Valley was born, and money poured into U.S. financial markets from around the world. A new group of companies emerged as leaders of the revitalized economy: Microsoft, Compaq, Cisco, Genentech, AOL, and Intel are excellent examples.

During the 1980s the United States also began to live on borrowed money. A trade deficit emerged with China in 1985. Since then, the balance of trade has been distinctly negative with the U.S. importing hundreds of billions of dollars more than it exports. The difference is made up by selling debt. Foreign investors buy U.S. Treasuries; the money flows through the banking system to consumers who take out loans so that they can buy foreign products. Foreign countries then recycle the money by purchasing more debt from the U.S. government. These dynamics enable the same dollars to flow through the economy many times—a dangerous situation that has alarmed economists for many years.

During the 1980s and 1990s, however, economic growth was strong enough to overcome the risks associated with deficit spending. Each new public offering brought new opportunity, and foreign capital poured into U.S. financial markets fueling the tenfold increase previously mentioned. The sharpest increase came with the birth and explosive growth of the internet between

1995 and 2000. Investors jumped on every new opportunity and stock valuations soared to unheard of levels. In 2000, the bubble collapsed, and the market fell erasing trillions of dollars of value.

Since then, world financial markets have undergone an amazing transformation. The dot-com collapse began on March 10, 2000, and continued until the NASDAQ Composite index bottomed out on October 9, 2002. The crash resulted from a technology bubble that grew out of control with stocks trading at absurdly high values completely unrelated to business performance. At the top, just before the crash, the NASDAQ Composite index was priced at 5048.86; when the bottom was reached in October 2002, the index had fallen 78% to 1114.11. In 2010 when these words were written, it traded around 2300—far less than half its former high.

The dot-com crash signaled the end of an era that was characterized by America's dominance of world financial markets. For the first time in more than 100 years, the "next big thing" cannot be identified. The manufacturing boom visible in the left half of Figure 5.2 depended on the availability of cheap energy and natural resources. America dominated because it was the only country unscathed by the war, and it had huge stores of natural resources including oil. The tenfold growth visible in the right half of the chart resulted from one simple discovery: the semiconducting properties of silicon. This important discovery enabled the invention of the transistor and ultimately the integrated circuit—essential components of every technical achievement from gene cloning to browsing the internet. Again the United States dominated and capitalized on technical achievements by attracting foreign investment capital.

Unfortunately, the industries launched during this era—biotech, computers, and mobile wireless—have all matured beyond their rapid growth phase. The venture capital community is suffering because it was initially designed around these opportunities. Some venture firms have even returned money to their investors because they are having problems finding the kinds of growth opportunities that fueled their business during the boom. Investment groups that had the foresight to identify such diverse business opportunities as gene cloning, stem cell research, mobile wireless, internet search, spreadsheets, databases, portable computers, digital cameras, and satellite radio often struggle to find new opportunities in the post dot-com world.

At the same time, the balance of power has shifted with China's emergence as a financial superpower. The United States no longer represents the "only game in town." Worse still, it appears to be behind or absent from many emerging technical markets. Figures 5.3 and 5.4 are designed to illustrate the dramatic difference between pre- and post-dot-com equity markets. Figure 5.3 displays the Dow from January 1985 to January 2000; Figure 5.4 begins at the end of the dot-com era and continues through the crash to June 2010 when this chapter was composed.

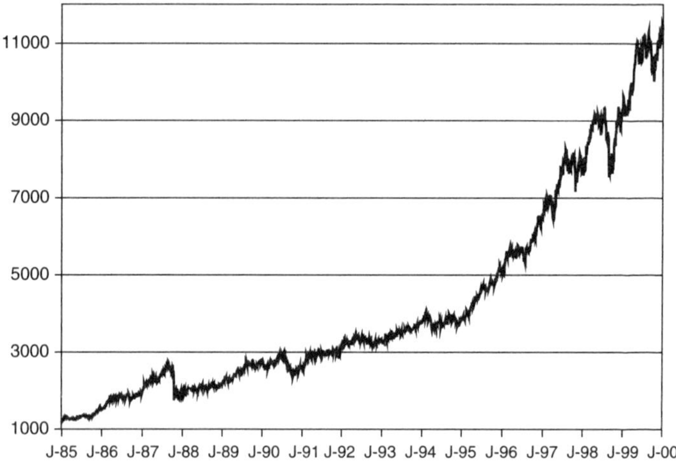

FIGURE 5.3 *Daily closing prices for the Dow Jones Industrial Average—January 1985 to January 2000. The Dow is represented on a linear scale (y-axis); dates are marked on the x-axis.*

FIGURE 5.4 *Daily closing prices for the Dow Jones Industrial Average—January 2000 to June 2010. The Dow is represented on a linear scale (y-axis); dates are marked on the x-axis.*

Not surprisingly, Figures 5.3 and 5.4 are strikingly different. They depict the behavior of the stock market during two distinctly different time frames. The financial boom evident in Figure 5.3 is strong enough to diminish the impact of every market correction. Figure 5.4 provides a sharp contrast because the entire period is dominated by financial corrections. January through March 2000 is characterized by volatile pre-crash behavior. The dot-com correction is next followed by a recovery that returns the market to its pre-crash high above 11,000 in early 2006.

The dot-com crash was unique for several reasons. Most significantly, it marked the beginning of a new era characterized by large, unpredictable swings in the financial markets. By late 2007, the Dow had risen another 27% to more than 14,000. The noise evident near the top of this peak is another example of pre-crash behavior. At this point a new financial bubble—the housing market—collapsed. The housing problem was complex because it also involved a banking collapse driven by reckless investing in complex credit derivatives related to the mortgage market. Ironically, the underlying cause was emergency level interest rates originally put in place to stimulate the economy. At this point the U.S. government decided to borrow and print enormous amounts of money while taking interest rates to 0%. A new rally was born and the Dow climbed 59%. Finally, at the right side of Figure 5.4, a 1,000-point decline was triggered by a debt crisis sweeping across several European countries including Portugal, Italy, Ireland, Greece, and Spain. The current era is marked by bubbles that are larger and closer together in time than ever before.

Other Recent Corrections

Figure 5.2 contains many corrections. As previously described, however, the upward growth of the market was strong enough to eclipse each correction with a new period of exponential growth. For example, in 1957, less than 3 years after the market fully recovered from the crash of '29, a new bubble began to emerge as money poured into electronics companies that were experiencing explosive growth during the dawn of the space age. Most had names that ended in "tron" or "onics"—Astron, Dutron, Vulcatron, Circuitronics, Videotronics, and Powertron Ultrasonics, just to name a few. They were the dot-com companies of the post-war era. None of them still exist.

Huge demand for relatively thin initial public offerings caused these stocks to soar when they were launched. As with internet companies, investors argued that tronics stocks could not be valued using traditional metrics because they represented the dawn of a new era. As a result, tronics stocks often traded at 50, 100, or even 200 times earnings. In 1962 the bubble burst taking the Dow from its December 1961 peak of 739 to a June low of 535—a 6-month, 28% correction. Although modest by today's standards, the correction did severe damage to portfolios that contained a large percentage of these stocks because, as just mentioned, many of the most popular companies failed to survive. In this regard, it is important to note that the NASDAQ crash of 2000 had a similar, but larger and more prolonged, effect on the Dow, taking the value down 38% from its December 1999 peak of 11,723 to an October 2002 low of 7286.

The market experienced other large, but brief, corrections prior to the 2000 crash. The first came in October 1987 and lasted just 10 trading days. It took the Dow from 2640 to 1738 erasing 34% of the market's value. Although the market began rising immediately, it took 2 years for the Dow to regain its pre-crash level.

Another correction came 3 years later in 1990 when a currency crisis in Japan signaled the end of the post-World War II bull market that had become a significant financial bubble in the Japanese market. The genesis of the correction was a forced appreciation of the yen. Japan's export-driven growth in the 1970s and 1980s created trade conflicts with other countries, most notably the United States. In September 1985, the Group of Five (G-5) finance ministers intervened to cause the Japanese yen to appreciate against the U.S. dollar. The value of the yen more than doubled in dollar terms over 3 years, from 251 yen per dollar in December 1984 to 121 yen per dollar in December 1987.

Substantial appreciation of the yen had a depressing effect on exports, and the Japanese economy went into a recession. The Bank of Japan lowered the discount rate while the government increased spending and introduced new tax cuts. These attempts at economic stimulus fuelled a speculative investment boom in real estate and stocks both in the domestic Japanese market and overseas because of the strength of the yen. When speculation became intense, the Bank of Japan became nervous about inflation. It responded by raising interest rates from a low of 2.5% in February 1987 to 4.25% at the end of 1989. Rates were increased twice more in 1990 to 6%. Stock prices responded by tumbling after their peak at the end of 1989.

The currency crisis in Japan rippled through world financial markets causing a significant correction in the U.S. stock market. Between July 16 and October 11 the Dow fell 21% from 3,000 to 2,365. The correction ended abruptly and the Dow rallied to close above 2,800 by February. It closed above its pre-correction level of 3,000 on April 17, 1991. Meanwhile Japan fell into a deep recession from which it never completely emerged. Twenty years later, at the time of this writing, Japanese interest rates remain near zero, and its stock market trades more than 72% below its December 1989 high of 38,957.

The Japanese crisis has many important lessons. First, it demonstrates the potential global impact of a currency crisis in one country. Another large drawdown began with an Asian financial crisis in July 1997. The correction in Asia caused commodity prices to fall triggering a second crisis in countries whose economies depended heavily on exporting oil, natural gas, metals, and lumber. Most affected was Russia where these products accounted for more than 80% of all exports. The situation ultimately causes a currency crisis that rippled through world financial markets. An unexpected but significant result was the collapse of a large U.S. hedge fund—Long-Term Capital Management (LTCM). The fund, which was highly leveraged to these markets, engaged in complex arbitrage trades that could not easily be unwound. It ultimately lost $4.6 billion and was bailed out by major creditors to avoid a wider collapse in the financial markets. The 1998 financial crisis and LTCM collapse triggered a 19% correction in the Dow, which fell from 9296 on July 20 to 7539 on August 31. The correction was completely reversed by late November.

Cause Versus Symptom

The Long-Term Capital correction appears as a noticeable dip near the right side of Figure 5.3 during the steepest part of the dot-com bubble when every correction was still a buying opportunity. Like the previous corrections, it had a definite bottom that represented a buying opportunity to even the most conservative investors. The dot-com crash was different. For many of the companies involved, there was no bottom, or the bottom was so low that that the remaining investors simply left their money in the stock on the speculation that it might rise again someday. Sun Microsystems, the company that put the dot in dot-com, is certainly one of the most prominent examples. Its stock soared to a split-adjusted price of $258 before crashing into the single digits destroying nearly $120 billion of market capitalization. Analysts issued strong buy recommendations and higher price targets for Sun even as the price crossed $250. Investors who purchased the stock in 1994, and held it through the rise and fall, experienced a 100x gain followed by a 98% loss. In October 2008, the stock traded for just $3.17.[1]

Sun Microsystems was not a cause of the dot-com collapse, it was a symptom. Unfortunately, stock analysts and the investing public tend to assume an endless trajectory of success for a company when it appears to be "on a roll." They proclaim that the soaring price reflects future earnings when in reality it is driven by the dynamics of short-covering and momentum investing, the latter being tightly linked to unrealistic investor optimism and the results of technical charting. We will return to a detailed discussion of this phenomenon and its dangers in the next section.

In the current era, crashes end only when governments step in and stop them with massive stimulus packages and emergency-level interest rates. This dynamic has set a new tone for the market's behavior. But a much more subtle and significant change has emerged from the technology boom of the past 20 years in the form of supercomputer-driven algorithmic trading.

Characteristics of the New Era

Students of the market often make the mistake of believing that today's automated trading systems are similar to the program trading systems of a few years ago. They are not. Today's systems come in a variety of forms that exploit technologies unavailable just a few years ago. High-frequency trading, the most significant force, has emerged as a new theme that dominates today's electronic marketplace.

High-frequency trading occurs when complex algorithms running on ultrafast computers scour the markets for tiny advantages that can be used to generate a profit. High-frequency trades often occur in less than a second and generate profits that are too small to be of any value to a private investor—in many cases less than a single penny. In total, however, these trades can move as many as a billion shares a day as programs repeatedly jump in and out of stocks across different exchanges.

High-frequency systems can also confound other investors by issuing and then canceling orders in time frames as small as a few thousandths of a second. They use this strategy to test the market and discover its tolerance for paying inflated prices. Small price differences are important because a few cents multiplied millions of times across hundreds of stocks can generate enormous profits.

High-frequency trading is only one of many themes in the supercomputer-driven financial world. Other approaches involve programs that follow trends in the millisecond time frame and are designed to prey on each other. Large financial institutions worry about the physical location of these machines because propagation delays across the internet might prevent these time-critical algorithms from functioning properly. The solution has been to locate systems at the exchange where they have immediate access to the trading queue and streams of information from different financial markets. It is not surprising to discover that the speed of electricity can be a problem in a world where algorithmic trading sometimes accounts for more than 80% of the total volume seen on an exchange. Joseph M. Mecane of NYSE Euronext said it best in a 2009 interview: "It's become a technological arms race, and what separates winners and losers is how fast they can move."

One of the most important characteristics of the new era is the speed with which a trend disappears. Before the financial landscape was ruled by computers, skilled technical analysts could identify and catch the beginning of a trend. Those days are gone. In today's market, any short-term trend that emerges, no matter how subtle, is instantly identified, exploited, and extinguished by a computer program. These activities themselves generate new opportunities that are also identified and exploited. Eventually, after a few minutes, the entire series of events melts back into statistical randomness, and the market resumes its original direction driven by economic fundamentals and news.

Figure 5.5 reveals these dynamics with a 3-minute tick-level chart of the SPDR Trust exchange traded fund (ticker: SPY) on June 6, 2010. The points on the chart are separated by 10 ticks with each tick representing a single price change. The chart is composed of 1,174 points or a total of 11,740 discreet price changes across 3 minutes. If we increased the resolution to 1 tick (1 price change per point), the chart would be limited to just 18 seconds (approximately 65 price changes per second). During the 3 minutes displayed, 10,990 shares changed hands.

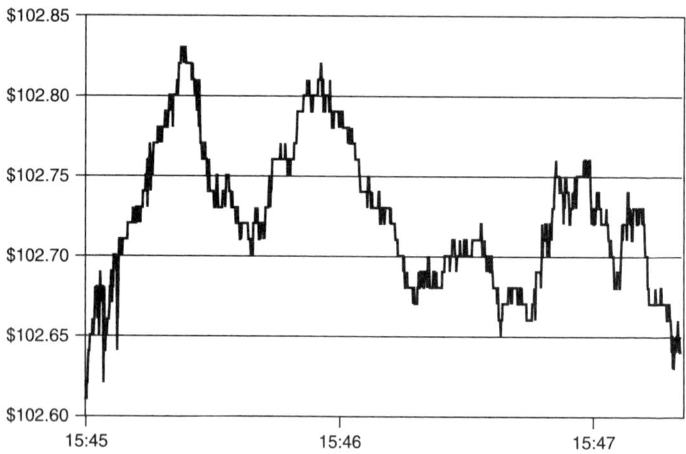

FIGURE 5.5 *Tick-level chart for SPDR Trust ETF (ticker: SPY) on June 6, 2010 between 15:45 and 15:48. Each point marks the close after 10 ticks with each tick representing a discreet price change. The 3 minute chart includes 11,740 individual price change ticks.*

Today's automated systems can collect and analyze information from several different financial markets and make trading decisions in the space of a single tick. Figure 5.5, however, reveals significant opportunities in much longer time frames. For example, the first rally that begins at 15:45 delivers more than $0.20 in 20 seconds—an eternity by algorithmic trading standards. The turnaround during the final 1/3 of the minute delivers another $0.10. A good algorithmic system would, therefore, deliver at least $0.30 during the first minute of the chart. Better systems would also capture a few cents from the mid-minute correction.

Buried in this chart, in the form of a series of disappearing trends, is a much more important and subtle message about the power of algorithmic trading. The tick-level activities just described have a significant impact on the market because they erase trends almost immediately. The most obvious example is the rally that begins at the left side of the chart and ends 20 seconds later. Although it is tempting to dismiss this activity as random noise, the number of price changes and total share volume suggest otherwise. A close look reveals that several trends begin during the time frame of the chart; each is rapidly extinguished by the market.

These dynamics have important implications. In the modern world, they redefine market efficiency and the meaning of the term "technical trend." Long-term trends that appear on traditional stock charts are nothing more than the collective remnants of the outcomes of millions of very short-lived rallies and declines like those in Figure 5.5. Individual investors, however, are generally unaware of the algorithmic trades that build and erase these trends because the time frames they track and can effectively react to are much longer. This effect puts investors at a tremendous disadvantage by exposing them to risks that they cannot react to in time frames that are much shorter than the time horizons of their trades. The situation was considerably different just a few years ago when investors' charts and program trading systems had similar time horizons. Today they are totally out of sync.

These dynamics tend to invalidate most forms of technical charting because, in effect, algorithmic trading systems operate under the radar. Simply stated, activities that occur at the tick level cannot be analyzed using minute, hour, or daily charts. Trends that appear on these charts are either the result of large-scale economic forces or artifacts with no predictive value. The overall effect of high-frequency trading has been to place private investors looking at stock charts completely out of sync with the underlying forces driving the market.

Differences between the current era and the past can be illustrated using relatively straightforward comparisons. One way is to measure the likelihood of one price change following another—up followed by up, or down followed by down. We can choose any time frame from single minutes to days, weeks, or months. Tables 5.1 and 5.2 display the results of such a comparison using daily price changes across time frames of 2 years for the S&P500. Table 5.1 covers the interval between July 2008 and July 2010; Table 5.2 covers 2 years between January 1995 and January 1997.

The data is organized into columns as follows: column 1 contains a threshold for the first day's price change; columns 2 and 3 list the percentage of up or down days that exceed the threshold; column 4 lists the percent chance of an up day exceeding the threshold being followed by another up day; columns 5–7 repeat this analysis for up followed by down, down followed by down, or down followed by up. For example, the third line of Table 5.1 reveals that 24% of all trading days closed up more than 1%. It also shows that the market closed down 25% of the time. For up days that exceeded the 1% threshold, the chance of the next day also closing higher was 48% (up-up). Conversely, after closing up more than 1%, the market had a 52% chance of reversing direction and closing down.

TABLE 5.1 *Percent Chance That One Daily Price Change Will Follow Another for the S&P500 Between July 2008 and July 2010 (Column 1 lists the chance of a single day exceeding the threshold in either the up or down direction. Columns 4–7 list probabilities for each of the four possible combinations where the first day exceeds the threshold and day 2 continues or reverses the direction.)*

Threshold	Up	Dwn	Up-Up	Up Dwn	Dwn-Dwn	Dwn-Up
0.0%	54%	46%	49%	51%	41%	59%
0.5%	36%	33%	52%	48%	44%	56%
1.0%	24%	25%	48%	52%	45%	55%
2.0%	11%	13%	42%	58%	39%	61%
3.0%	6%	8%	34%	66%	42%	58%

TABLE 5.2 *Percent Chance That One Daily Price Change Will Follow Another for the S&P500 Between January 1995 and January 1997 (Column 1 lists the chance of a single day exceeding the threshold in either the up or down direction. Columns 4–7 list probabilities for each of the four possible combinations where the first day exceeds the threshold and day 2 continues or reverses the direction.)*

Threshold	Up	Dwn	Up-Up	Up-Dwn	Dwn-Dwn	Dwn-Up
0.0%	0.58	0.41	0.61	0.38	0.46	0.54
0.5%	0.24	0.13	0.63	0.36	0.52	0.48
1.0%	0.06	0.04	0.71	0.29	0.63	0.37

The tables are strikingly different. Most significant is the lack of 2% and 3% thresholds in the 1995–1997 data (Table 5.2). These lines were omitted because the number of events was statistically insignificant. There were no up days and only 3 down days (0.6%) that exceeded the 2% threshold; only 1 down day exceeded the 3% threshold. Conversely, in the more recent time frame of Table 5.1, 11% of up days and 13% of down days exceeded the 2% threshold (57 up days and 66 down days, respectively).

Another significant difference exists with regard to the probability of one day following the next. At the 1% threshold level, for example, the chance of an up day being followed by a second up day is 71% in the 1995–1997 time frame, but random (48%) in the 2008–2010 time frame. This difference is consistent with the observation that the current market is more efficient than the market of 15 years ago, and that this increased efficiency works to rapidly erase emerging trends. Moreover, the 3% threshold line in Table 5.2 reveals a tendency for large price changes to reverse. This tendency, often referred to as mean reversion, has become the basis for a variety of complex trading strategies.

In the next section we see that the tendency for today's market to erase trends persists at all levels down to individual minutes. The data is consistent with the behavior illustrated in Figure 5.5.

Problems with Technical Analysis in the Modern Era

Technical analysis depends on a variety of basic calculations to identify meaningful chart patterns that can be used to predict the direction that a stock is likely to take. The standard tools include an endless variety of moving average combinations in addition to measures of volume, momentum, and rate of change. Technical traders have, for years, depended on these indicators to help them time the market and predict its direction. They usually track several at a time in an effort to glean new information that the market has yet to discover.

Regardless of the specific approach being used, technical analysis is always based on the assumption that the recent price history of a stock contains information that can be used to predict its future direction. This belief is grounded in the assumption that the market is inefficient. It also implies that an investor drawing lines on a stock chart can compete with an army of supercomputers that have far more information and can react millions of times faster.

The power of these systems is apparent in the description of a collaborative project launched in 2009 by IBM and TD Securities.[2, 3] The project's ambitious goal is the development of the world's most powerful algorithmic trading system. The new approach enables rapid, intelligent analysis of live streaming data from a large number of sources. It combines supercomputing horsepower with advanced data stream management software to cope with information volumes that often exceed two million messages per second. As with any automated trading system, the goal is to reduce the time between the receipt of market data and the final trading decision. By achieving lower latency and higher data rates, the new system can respond to market situations before they can be detected by other institutional investors. Stated differently, the IBM/TD Securities system is designed to absorb more data, make better decisions, and operate in shorter time frames than any other automated system. More important, it sets a new standard of market efficiency and further reduces the possibility of finding a predictive pattern in a stock chart.

We can verify that high performance tick-by-tick trading extinguishes trends almost instantly by studying the statistics of single-minute price changes. A simple test is to count the number of up minutes that are followed by another up minute over a relatively long period of time. If trends exist, they should be apparent in the behavior of a stock after a large initial price change. Minutes with the largest price changes should be followed by continued movement in the same direction. If no clear relationship can be found between a large price change in 1 minute and movement in the next, then there is no trend.

Table 5.3 displays the results of such an experiment. A single stock, Apple Computer (ticker: AAPL), was used because it is highly liquid and traded both by private investors and institutions. Results were compiled using 1 year (252 trading days) of minute-by-minute prices. The complete data set includes 98,085 individual minutes. The first column of the table contains threshold data for the first minute. In all cases, the second minute has no threshold because we are seeking only its direction.

TABLE 5.3 *Number of Minutes Repeating the Direction of a Previous Minute for 1 Year of Apple Computer Stock (The first column indicates the threshold used to filter the first minute. The data spans 98,085 trading minutes.[4])*

Min#1 Chng.	Min#1 Up	Min#2 Up	Min#2 Dwn	Min#2 Same	Up-Up Avg	Up-Dwn Avg	Up-Same Avg
0.0%	47,543	22,178	23,818	1,547	46.6%	50.1%	3.3%
0.1%	18,925	8,707	9,743	475	46.0%	51.5%	2.5%
0.2%	7,143	3,286	3,710	147	46.0%	51.9%	2.1%
0.3%	3,116	1,433	1,634	49	46.0%	52.4%	1.6%
0.4%	1,552	703	827	22	45.3%	53.3%	1.4%
0.5%	826	363	453	10	43.9%	54.8%	1.2%
0.6%	469	207	258	4	44.1%	55.0%	0.9%
0.7%	291	128	160	3	44.0%	55.0%	1.0%
0.8%	176	74	100	2	42.0%	56.8%	1.1%
0.9%	115	53	61	1	46.1%	53.0%	0.9%
1.0%	80	42	37	1	52.5%	46.3%	1.3%
1.1%	47	26	20	1	55.3%	42.6%	2.1%
1.2%	30	18	11	1	60.0%	36.7%	3.3%
1.3%	23	15	8	0	65.2%	34.8%	0.0%
1.4%	17	11	6	0	64.7%	35.3%	0.0%
1.5%	15	9	6	0	60.0%	40.0%	0.0%
1.6%	8	5	3	0	62.5%	37.5%	0.0%
1.7%	6	3	3	0	50.0%	50.0%	0.0%
1.8%	6	3	3	0	50.0%	50.0%	0.0%
1.9%	6	3	3	0	50.0%	50.0%	0.0%
2.0%	6	3	3	0	50.0%	50.0%	0.0%

No clear correlation emerges at any level in the table; even the largest single-minute price changes did not result in persistent trends. This phenomenon is most apparent at the bottom where a severe first minute change threshold of 2% reduces the number of events to just 6 (0.006% of the total number of minutes). Of these 6 events, 3 were followed by a second up minute. It is surprising that only half of the following minutes closed higher because these events are highly unusual and almost certainly represent special situations caused by news surprises. At a slightly lower but still very rare threshold of 1.5%, the results are similar—only 9 of 15 minutes followed in the same direction. The slight increase to 60% is not statistically significant because the number of events is vanishingly small.

It is also important to recognize that data for the most extreme minutes can be distorted by order imbalances and filled trading queues—situations that often take more than a single minute to resolve. Volume data supports this assertion. The average volume for the unusual minutes near the bottom of the table is 6.4x that of a typical minute.

One way to be more specific in our search is to study situations in which a trend appears to be emerging. A simple approach is to follow a stock's behavior immediately after a pair of minutes where minute #2 follows the direction of minute #1. Table 5.4 outlines the results of such an experiment. It displays 3-minute data across the complete range of thresholds. As before, the first column lists the change threshold for minute #1. The second column, labeled Min#1-#2 Up Test counts the number of events where minute #1 was up more than the threshold amount, and minute #2 also closed higher. The three columns that follow contain data about the direction of the third minute—up, same, or down. Instances where minute #3 closed "up" represent a continuation of the trend initiated during the first 2 minutes. The probabilities associated with these continuations are listed in the final column at the right side of the table.

TABLE 5.4 ***Behavior of Minute #3 After an Uptrend Established During Minutes #1 and #2 (In each case, minute #1 must exceed the change threshold listed in column 1, and minute #2 must continue the uptrend by closing higher than minute #1. Data spans 98,085 trading minutes of Apple Computer stock.[5])***

Min#1 Chng.	Min#1-#2 Up Test	Min#3 Up	Min#3 Same	Min#3 Down	Min#3 Up%
0.0%	22105	10121	707	11277	45.8%
0.1%	8674	3948	207	4519	45.5%
0.2%	3274	1480	67	1727	45.2%
0.3%	1428	661	14	753	46.3%
0.4%	700	335	6	359	47.9%
0.5%	362	181	3	178	50.0%
0.6%	206	95	1	110	46.1%
0.7%	127	61	1	65	48.0%
0.8%	74	39	0	35	52.7%
0.9%	53	24	0	29	45.3%
1.0%	42	21	0	21	50.0%

The data contains absolutely no evidence of a continuing uptrend. Even the very rare 2-minute events near the bottom of the table lack the power to initiate an uptrend that persists into minute #3. At the 1% level (last line of the table), these events occur only 0.04% of the time. Repeating this experiment in the reverse direction by selecting pairs of down minutes yields nearly identical results—that is, 2-minute down trends do not persist into minute #3.

These dynamics are symptomatic of a market dominated by powerful computers trading in time frames that make a minute seem like eternity. To test this hypothesis we need to study the time frame these machines are trading in. If our hypothesis is correct, then we should see statistical evidence of trends at the tick level where they cannot be erased by normal market forces. Conversely, if our analysis reveals a total lack of predictability at this level, then billions of dollars are being wasted on supercomputing infrastructure because the markets are totally random and efficient at all levels.

Table 5.5 contains the results of a simple, but revealing experiment. As before, each line represents data for a different threshold. For clarity, because this analysis counts individual ticks as small as a single penny, the threshold is measured as a change greater than or equal to the value in column 1. (For example, the first line sets a price change threshold of greater than or equal to $0.01.) Because $0.01 is the smallest possible price change for a stock, the threshold listed in line 1 maintains its previous meaning as "any change."

TABLE 5.5 *Percent Chance of a Single Tick Price Change Repeating the Direction of the Previous Change for 60,000 Ticks of Apple Computer Stock (The first column indicates the threshold used to filter the first tick [values in $0.01]. Note: Threshold is measured as >= the value in column 1.[6])*

Tick#1 Chng. ($)	Tick#1 Up	Tick#2 Up	Up-Up Avg.	Tick#1 Dwn	Tick#2 Dwn	Dwn-Dwn Avg.
0.01	12100	4164	34.4%	12187	4251	34.9%
0.02	9497	3212	33.8%	9568	3302	34.5%
0.03	2921	865	29.6%	2864	893	31.2%
0.04	2037	592	29.1%	2026	604	29.8%
0.05	716	194	27.1%	711	193	27.1%
0.06	274	75	27.4%	285	76	26.7%
0.07	216	57	26.4%	214	60	28.0%
0.08	123	34	27.6%	120	28	23.3%
0.09	69	16	23.2%	65	17	26.2%
0.10	54	13	24.1%	49	13	26.5%
0.11	25	6	24.0%	30	6	20.0%

Because each tick is an individual transaction, many ticks can occur at the same price. Transactions occurring at the same price are referred to as zero plus or zero minus ticks. A zero plus tick occurs when the execution price is the same as the previous transaction, but greater than the most recent trade at a different price. For example, if a series of trades executes at $50.01, $50.05, and $50.05, the last trade is the zero plus tick because it executed at the same price as the previous transaction, but higher than the preceding tick of $50.01. A zero minus tick is the reverse; the execution price remains the same as the last trade but lower than the most recent trade at a different price.

The zero plus/zero minus effect is enhanced by programs that split trades into many smaller pieces. Institutional traders often use such programs to disguise very large transactions that can affect the market they are attempting to trade in. For example, a trade to sell 10,000 shares of a stock at $50 is often entered into the queue as 100 trades of 100 shares at a price of $50. These trades will ultimately generate 100 identically priced ticks or transactions. It is also common for the trading queue to contain many different sets of trades that can be matched off at the same price. As these trades execute, multiple ticks are recorded at that price. The result is a flat spot on the tick-by-tick chart.

Because our goal is to study the impact of one price change on the next, zero plus and zero minus ticks were removed from the data presented in Table 5.5. For example, line 6 of the table should be interpreted to mean that the stock experienced 274 upticks greater than or equal to $0.06, and that the next price change continued in the same direction only 75 times (27.4%). Conversely, the next price change was a downtick 72.6% of the time.

The data reveals an increasing tendency for large price changes to trigger an immediate reversal. At the top of the table where the smallest price changes of just $0.01 are displayed, the chance of a continuation is just under 35% for both directions. Reversals, therefore, occur more than 65% of the time. Conversely, at the extreme end of the spectrum where 60,000 ticks yield only 25 upward and 30 downward price changes, the probability of the next tick continuing in the same direction is only 24% for upticks and 20% for downticks. The chance of a reversal, therefore, grows to 76% on the upside and 80% on the downside.

Not surprisingly, the results clearly support the emergence of trends at the tick level. These results are significant because the tick-by-tick analysis accurately tabulates all changes without the artificial constraint of time boundaries. The results uncover a region of very brief time frames and very small price changes where persistent trends cannot be erased by the market. This region of the very brief and very small has become the target for large financial institutions armed with the most powerful computers and software. Private investors are disadvantaged because they cannot trade in this time frame.

Summary

The goal of this chapter was to demonstrate that technical trends only emerge in very brief time frames where they cannot be erased by normal market forces. These activities can be seen on tick-level charts that track every price change without the constraints of time boundaries. In this environment where a minute seems like eternity, trends persist for just a few seconds before being extinguished by the actions of automated trading systems. These dynamics represent a new level of efficiency that places private investors at an extreme disadvantage.

Our discussion revealed that the chance of a 1-minute price change repeating the direction of the previous minute is random. Moreover, this randomness persists even when the first minute of the sequence experiences a very large price change. We also examined situations where a large price change persisted for 2 minutes and discovered that the direction of the third minute was random. This second test was designed to filter out less significant events and focus on situations where a clear trend was beginning to emerge. Other tests, not reported here, extended the analysis to several minutes, hours, and days, across a variety of stocks and indexes. The results were always the same.

These dynamics change at the individual tick level where algorithmic trading systems open and close trades faster than private investors can react. The statistical evidence for trends at this level is unmistakable.

For example, in the 60,000 tick case study of Apple Computer presented in Table 5.5, the largest single tick downward price changes of $0.11 had an 80% chance of reversing on the next tick. The same size upward price change occurred slightly less often and had a 76% chance of immediate reversal. These numbers are both statistically significant and important because they are the footprints left by algorithmic trading systems that are capable of buying on one tick and selling on the next. For these systems a few seconds is a long time to hold a trade.

In many ways these dynamics represent the death of technical charting as it was once known. Yesterday's simple chart patterns and indicators are no longer relevant because the direction of the market results from the accumulated activities of thousands of computers operating at the single tick level. Simple charting and analysis tools cannot measure and track these activities.

Fortunately, while this bleak assessment might tend to invalidate traditional technical charting, it leaves in place all kinds of trading opportunities for private investors. It is important to remember that algorithmic trading systems do not remove the large-scale forces driving the economy and individual stocks. Those opportunities are as abundant as ever. The late 2000s weak dollar trend that took gold from $400 to $1200 could not be extinguished by algorithmic trading because it was driven by large-scale political and economic forces. These forces transcend the behavior of algorithmic trading systems. However, gold investors who relied on short-term chart patterns and technical indicators made a huge mistake because they were competing against a more powerful opponent with better tools and information. Worse still, the chart patterns they were looking at were being created by the very systems they were trading against.

Endnotes

1. After the NASDAQ crash, Sun Microsystems stock traded around $3. It eventually rallied above $5. On November 12, 2007, Sun Microsystems executed a four-for-one reverse stock split that raised the share price from $5.14 to more than $20. It continued falling, however, and in April 2009, Oracle acquired Sun for $9.50 per share. The acquisition cost was $7.5 billion.

2. "IBM Unveils Prototype of Fast Financial Analysis System." *Automated Trader*, April 14, 2009.

3. "IBM Unveils Prototype of World's Fastest Financial Analysis System." IBM press release, April 9, 2009.

4. Jeff Augen, *Day Trading Options*, Pearson Education, 2010, Ch. 2, Table 2.1. Opening minutes are not used in this analysis because, in each case, the previous trading minute occurred 17 hours earlier at the previous day's close.

5. Jeff Augen, *Day Trading Options*, Pearson Education, 2010, Ch. 2, Table 2.4.

6. Jeff Augen, *Day Trading Options*, Pearson Education, 2010, Ch. 2, Table 2.11.

Chapter 6

The Importance of Volatility

Introduction

Option traders understand the central role of volatility because it is the principal component of every option price. Ask an option trader to compare different stocks trading at different prices, and he will immediately ask what the underlying volatility is for each. Traders routinely use this information to predict the likelihood of certain size price changes in specific time frames.

Recent years have seen an explosion in the use of volatility calculations as a measure of risk across individual sectors and the broad market. As a result, the Chicago Board Options Exchange Volatility Index (VIX) has evolved into one of the most closely followed indicators available today. Most traders can quote the value of the VIX at any time during any trading day if they are watching the market.

This chapter introduces basic volatility calculations in the context of price change behavior. It also reveals a new approach to using volatility comparisons to predict large market corrections. The discussion is designed to be accessible to any investor, and every attempt has been made to minimize the amount of math used in the descriptions. Readers who are not familiar with the basics of put and call options are encouraged to visit Appendix A, "Options Primer."

Fooled by Randomness

Chapter 5, "A New Era," made the case that today's high-speed computer-driven markets are fundamentally different from those of a few years ago. This discussion was intended to highlight the dangers associated with using old tools to play a new game. It was also intended to highlight the widening gap between the power of large institutional investors and all the other market participants. Private investors are often fooled into believing they can compete. Much of this misconception is related to the rapid advance in desktop trading platforms, which now include sophisticated charting software and filtering tools for identifying specific trading opportunities. Unfortunately, as we saw in Chapter 5, these tools operate in time frames that are thousands of times too slow to compete with the large systems that drive the market. More important, private investors looking at patterns on stock charts are competing with the very systems that create and exploit those patterns. These issues matter because the market is a zero sum game in which an investor can only win money if another investor loses. Private investors can only take money out of the market if they can win against these powerful forces.

This discussion does not nullify the value of stock charts. However, it makes the point that technical charting has little value outside the context of financial news and the economy. Conversely, as we saw in Chapter 4, "Identifying Trends," decorating a stock chart with news items can bring focus and meaning to its up and down trends. News-annotated charts are also easier to understand because they highlight the difference between real trends and noise. Investors should avoid stocks whose behavior cannot be reconciled with the broad market and the news.

However, there was a time, not long ago, when a perceptive technical analyst could identify trading opportunities ahead of the market and independent of the news. It was even possible to discover new combinations of standard charting techniques that had enduring predictive power. These approaches spanned a broad spectrum of complexity from simple combinations of moving averages to advanced statistical functions for measuring the relative strength of different trends. Those days have passed. Traditional technical analysis, as a standalone approach, is no longer a viable weapon for the average investor.

Figure 6.1 highlights these issues with three different stock charts. Each displays a year of daily closing prices. Only two of the charts are real; the third was created by a random number generator. Can you spot the fake?

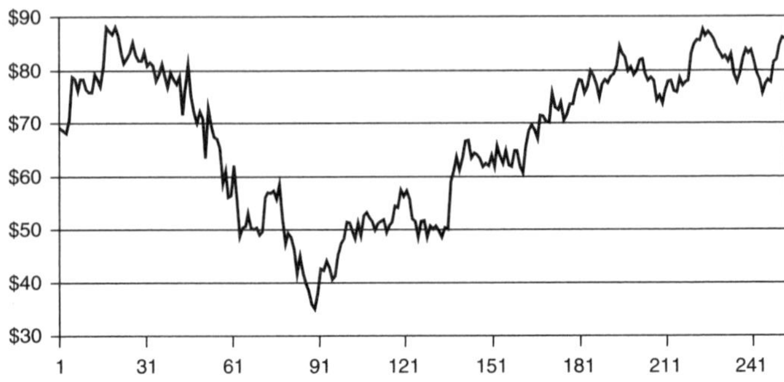

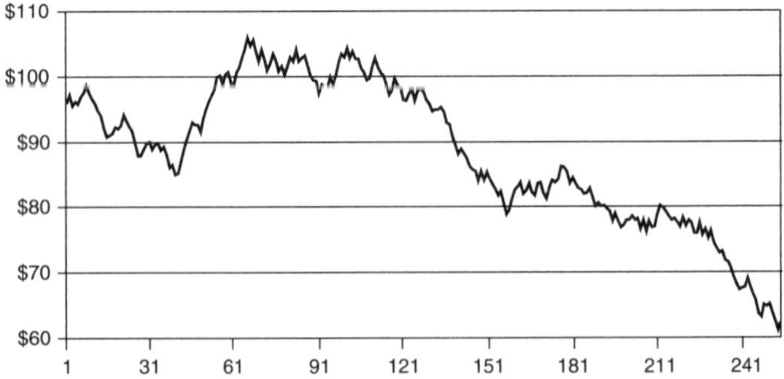

FIGURE 6.1 *Three stock charts displaying one year of daily closing prices: Amazon (top), Fedex (middle), and a third chart created by a random number generator (bottom). Days are displayed on the x-axis, price on the y-axis. There is no reliable way to spot the counterfeit chart.*

The fake chart was created by adding random numbers to an arbitrarily selected starting value. It contains many surprises. Most significant is the emergence of trends that span periods of days, even weeks. These trends would cancel each other if the chart were extended across thousands of data points; they would vanish completely if millions of points were used. But reducing the number of points to just a couple of hundred allows the emergence of completely random, but seemingly significant, trends. The lesson to be learned here is that complex patterns can emerge from simple random processes. Mathematicians have written extensively about this phenomenon—often in the context of binary events like the toss of a coin. These discussions generally illustrate that a coin tosser's winnings can rise or fall surprisingly far from the expected average of zero over hundreds, even thousands of tosses.[1] A second surprise is the extent to which technical analysis can succeed against random information. We can easily create a set of trading rules that delivers a solid profit from a random chart. This mistake, commonly referred to as *over fitting*, is the underlying cause of many misconceptions about technical analysis. The problem occurs when technical indicators are recursively tuned against a dataset until they deliver optimized results. Indicators that are over fitted to one dataset will not work against another.

The standard tools of technical analysis could be applied to any of the three charts with absolutely no hint of a problem. Figure 6.2 makes this point using the random stock chart from Figure 6.1. It includes two very simple indicators. The first is a 50-day moving average (solid gray line). The second is a channel marked by dotted gray lines that highlights a region of consistently lower highs and lower lows. This type of behavior is often considered a bearish indicator, especially when it follows a steep rally. Such a rally is visible near the left side of the chart where the stock climbs from $85 on day 40 to $105 on day 61. The peaks of the channel also define a resistance level around $105. The stock's failure to close above this resistance level combined with the steady decline and a cross below the 50-day moving average are all bearish signals.

FIGURE 6.2 *Emergence of a downtrend on a random stock chart. Dotted gray lines mark the emergence of a downtrend characterized by lower highs and lower lows. The solid gray line traces the 50-day moving average. An arrow marks the point where both indicators converge driving the decision to sell short.*

Our analysis was clearly correct because the stock proceeded to fall 40% over the next 100 days. But something must be wrong because the chart we analyzed was created by a random number generator. That said, there must be a way to distinguish the fake in Figure 6.1.

Studying Price Change Behavior

The answer is to decompose each of the three charts into a sequence of individual price changes. Although each example in Figure 6.1 contains recognizable features such as rallies, declines, and areas of support or resistance, the underlying price change data reveals fundamental differences that cannot be discerned by charting the price. These differences are displayed in Figure 6.3 where each change, represented as a vertical bar, is calculated as the percent increase or decrease from the previous closing price. In the new analysis, the counterfeit stock chart stands out from the others as a set of consistently small individual price changes that are symmetrically clustered around zero. These characteristics make perfect sense because the chart was created using a series of random numbers that vary within a small range. Within that range, all changes—large and small—are equally likely. Stated differently, a $2.00 price change is as likely as a $0.02 change. Each point in the random chart is also isolated from the others in the sense that the stock never moves in any particular direction. Up is always as likely as down because each change is an independent entity created by the random number generator.

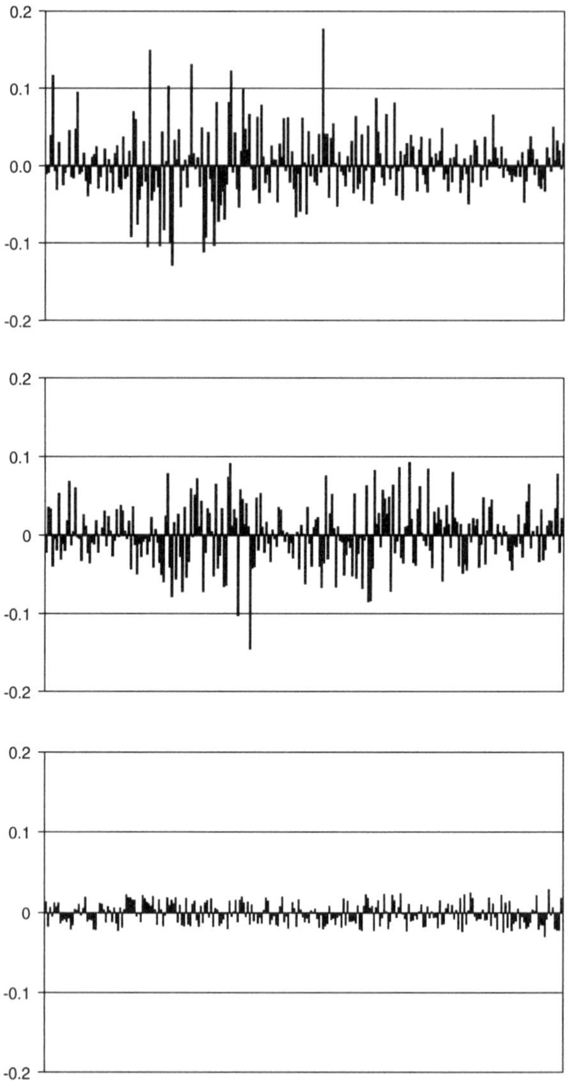

FIGURE 6.3 *Three stock charts from Figure 6.1 recast as a series of individual price changes. The fake chart, created by a random number generator, stands out from the others.*

Real stock charts are composed of a series of price changes that have no limitations with regard to size. However, the magnitude of the price changes fits a mathematical distribution where large changes are less likely than small ones. In the real world, a $2.00 price change is less likely than a $0.02 change. For example, in Figure 6.3, the chart displaying price changes for Amazon contains 228 price spikes larger than 0.5%, 185 larger than 1%, 42 larger than 5%, 11 that exceed 10%, and just 1 above 17%. These values fit a bell-shaped curve where the peak represents a small number of unusually large price changes. In the Amazon case, a single large price spike defines the peak of the bell curve. This spike is clearly visible in the top pane of Figure 6.3.

The synthetic chart is fundamentally different from the others because it is built on a perfectly flat distribution where, as previously stated, every size price spike is equally likely. The difference is apparent in Figure 6.3.

Price change distribution is the key to understanding the behavior of any financial instrument. For this reason, it forms the basis of all option pricing theory. With minor modifications, our experiment can become a springboard for this type of analysis. One difference is the method for measuring price change. In the option trading world, the logarithm of each price change is used instead of the percent change. The numbers are almost identical. For example, a move from $95 to $98 would represent an increase of 3.16%. If we calculate the change using the logarithm of 98/95, the answer would be 3.11.

Calculating Volatility

Volatility, the key component of any option price, is equal to the standard deviation of the price changes measured over a predefined period of time. (A 20-day window or 1 trading month is often used for daily price change calculations.) To calculate a stock's annual volatility, the standard deviation value is multiplied by an "annualization factor" equal to the square root of the number of trading days in one year. The most commonly accepted factor is 15.87, which is based on 252 trading days. A sample volatility calculation is displayed in Table 6.1.

TABLE 6.1 *Sample Volatility Calculation*

Close($)	Log Chng	Stdev	Volatility
69.12			
68.48	–0.0093		
67.97	–0.0075		
70.54	0.0371		
78.72	0.1097		
78.31	–0.0052		
75.98	–0.0302		
78.21	0.0289		
78.21	0.0000		
76.34	–0.0242		
75.75	–0.0078		
75.71	–0.0005		
79.11	0.0439		
78.09	–0.0130		
76.95	–0.0147		
80.51	0.0452		
88.09	0.0900		
87.25	–0.0096		
86.69	–0.0064		
88.03	0.0153		
86.40	–0.0187	0.0375	59.5%
83.11	–0.0388	0.0389	61.7%
81.29	–0.0221	0.0393	62.4%

Volatility calculations displayed in column 4 are based on a sliding window that spans 21 days or 20 price changes. The process can obviously be extended to any length table by continually sliding the window forward after each calculation. We can use this approach to create a chart that displays the volatility of each of our stocks across the one-year time frame in Figure 6.1. The results appear in Figure 6.4. Once again, Amazon and Fedex exhibit the kind of complex behavior that would be expected for a real stock. Volatility rises and falls over time in response to financial news and world events. More significantly, sharp declines during times of instability are characterized by rising volatility while rallies are usually marked by falling volatility. These dynamics are well known in the option trading world. The fake, however, exhibits no significant change in volatility over the entire one-year time frame.

These charts highlight the importance of studying price change behavior and volatility. An investor who studies stock charts using the standard tools of technical analysis would be unable to detect the fake. An option trader, however, would immediately know that something was wrong.

Option traders can also calculate the statistical chance of a certain size price spike for any stock if they know the price and volatility. This simple but powerful calculation allows the direct comparison of different stocks trading at different prices with different underlying volatilities. The method is relatively simple: Multiply the stock price by the annual volatility and divide by the square root of the number of time frames per year—sqrt(12) for a 1-month price change and sqrt(252) for a 1-day price change. The result is the value of a 1 standard deviation price change for the stated time frame. Standard deviations translate directly into probability. In statistical terms, 68% of all price changes can be expected to be smaller than 1 stdev, 87% will be smaller than 1.5 stdev, and 95% should be smaller than 2 stdev.

For a $100 stock with 30% volatility, a 1-day 1 standard deviation price change would be equal to $100 x 0.30 / sqrt(252) = $1.89. In probability terms, we would expect this stock to experience a price change larger than $1.89 approximately every third trading day (32% of the time).

We can extend the calculation to 1 month by replacing sqrt(252) with sqrt(12) or 3.46. The new result would, therefore, be $100 x 0.30 / 3.46 = $8.67. We would expect a price change larger than this amount approximately every third month. Doubling this value to $17.34 yields the value of a 2 stdev change. If option pricing theory is correct, this size price spike can be expected less than 5% of the time, or once in every 20 months for this particular stock.

Option traders have always used this approach to make decisions about strike prices and time frames for their trades. In recent years, however, volatility has become a key measure of the market's behavior for all investors. This interest has fueled the creation of a variety of volatility indexes for tracking both individual sectors and the broad market. By far, the most popular and closely followed is the Chicago Board Options Exchange (CBOE) Volatility Index commonly known as the VIX. This index, continually calculated by the CBOE, has become a standard benchmark of investor sentiment and market volatility. It can be displayed just like any other stock chart on a modern trading platform.

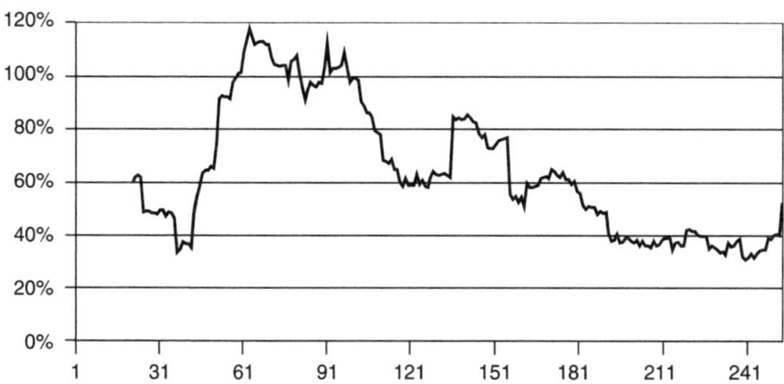

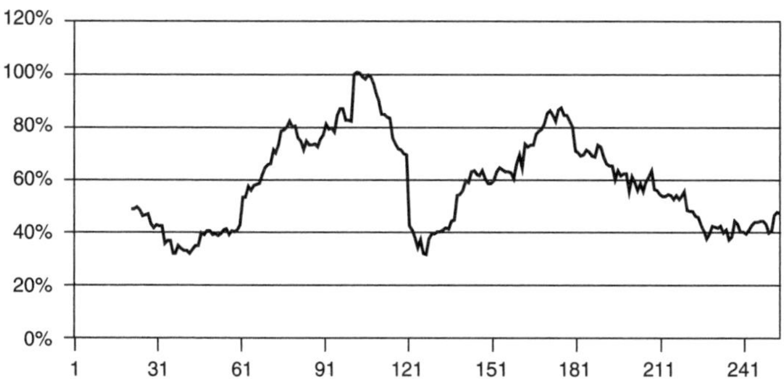

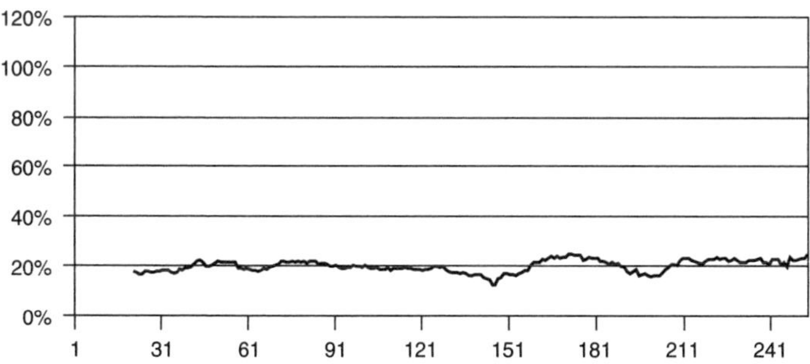

FIGURE 6.4 *Volatility charts for the three stocks in Figure 6.1.*

The CBOE Volatility Index

The value of the VIX is based on the implied volatility priced into S&P 500 index options. This approach to calculating the index distinguishes it from purely theoretical approaches. If, for example, option traders are concerned that the market is inching toward a correction, the actual trading prices of S&P 500 index options will rise. This increase will immediately be reflected in the value of the VIX. It is not necessary to be completely familiar with the details of the calculation to follow and understand the index. In simple terms, the VIX tends to rise when the market becomes unstable. Falling markets are unstable and, therefore, normally characterized by a rising VIX. This negative correlation between the VIX and the market is well documented.[2] The index can also be helpful as a leading indicator because it tends to rise near the end of a rally and fall when a downtrend is ending.

The VIX sometimes provides signals that can be used to predict the direction of the market. Especially relevant are differences between the value of the VIX and the actual volatility of the S&P 500. If, for example, the S&P 500 has been rising steadily for some time, its volatility may be unrealistically low with regard to the risk of a reversal. Investors anticipating a correction may bid up the price of S&P 500 index options so that implied volatility of the options is much higher than actual volatility of the underlying index. In such cases, the ratio of VIX to actual volatility is more important than the absolute values of either. Stated differently, the VIX can be reasonably low by historical standards but high in comparison to the market's true volatility.[3]

A New Indicator for Predicting Market Corrections

Having a method for calculating actual volatility allows us to calibrate the VIX against the market and track the ratio of the VIX to true volatility (VIX/true) over long periods of time. This experiment is also supported by decades of freely available historical data that the CBOE has posted on its website. All of the information can be downloaded in spreadsheet form with the click of a mouse. The comparison yields surprising results.

A spreadsheet was constructed with daily closing prices for both the VIX and the S&P 500 beginning in January 1999. This time frame was chosen because it predates the NASDAQ market crash by more than one year. Across the entire time frame of the study, approximately 3,000 trading days, the ratio averaged 1.3—that is, the VIX averaged 1.3x the underlying volatility of the S&P 500 calculated in a 20-day window. It climbed sharply only four times between the beginning of 1999 and 2010. During each of these events the ratio rose above 2.3.

The first three distortions were associated with various waves of the NASDAQ collapse. The fourth followed closely after, at the beginning of the recovery in September 2003. Following the fourth distortion, the market experienced four large oscillations over a nine-month time frame. During these oscillations the S&P climbed as high as 1150 and fell as low as 1060—a volatile time to say the least.

More important, each large spike in the VIX/true ratio was eventually followed by a reversal where the ratio fell to a value near 1. In each case, the low ratio signaled that the market had stabilized and the drawdown was over. Two additional examples preceded this writing by just a few months. The first occurred in January 2010, following an increase of the ratio to 2.1. The market fell sharply losing 8% of its value in just 15 trading days. As predicted, the decline ended when the ratio fell to 1. The ratio peaked again in late March at a value of 2.3, and the market began falling a few weeks later on April 23. The drawdown ended on June 7, with the market 13% lower, and the VIX/true ratio settling once again at a stable level of 1.1.

Figure 6.5 illustrates the VIX/true effect by tracing the S&P 500 through the NASDAQ meltdown. The first two arrows mark spikes above 2.3 in the VIX/true ratio; the third arrow marks a downward spike that occurred as the market began to stabilize. The chart begins on September 5, 2000, and ends on March 13, 2003.

FIGURE 6.5 *The S&P 500 during the NASDAQ meltdown. Significant spikes and low points in the VIX/true ratio are noted on the chart.*

Most investors mistakenly believe that a low VIX represents stability and a lack of fear in the market. Some analysts even refer to the VIX as a "fear" indicator. It's not that simple. The market dynamics of the first half of 2010 serve as an excellent example.

By April, the market had rallied more than 70% from its low of the previous year—a prolonged rally that resulted from a variety of financial stimulus packages funded through emergency-level interest rates and massive borrowing. Although the economy was fundamentally weak, bearish investors had given up being short because each downturn had been followed by a fierce short covering rally. On the other side, institutional investors were cautious about entering long positions at the end of such a long and powerful rally in a weak economy.

With few investors willing to risk being short and even fewer confident enough to remain long, trading volumes collapsed. Furthermore, the lack of committed long positions eliminated out-of-the-money put buyers who are normally willing to overpay for hedges against their positions. This particular dynamic drove down the value of the VIX, which ultimately bottomed out around 17. Simply stated, the index wasn't low because the market was safe; it was low because everyone was out. However, because the actual volatility of the market had fallen below 7.5%, the VIX/true ratio was still high and a sharp correction followed.

Trading Volatility

The VIX has become much more than an indicator. Many investors trade volatility in the form of VIX options, and almost every institutional investor uses some blend of VIX options and futures as a hedge against potential losses in their portfolio. Trading the VIX has become so popular that in 2009, Barclays Bank PLC launched a simple exchange-traded investment vehicle that tracks a blend of VIX futures contracts. Any investor can now buy and sell volatility as easily as a stock. There are two choices, VXX (short term) and VXZ (mid-term). Each is an Exchange Traded Note (ETN), an unsecured debt security that trades just like an ETF:[4]

- **iPath S&P 500 VIX Short-Term Futures ETN (VXX)**: Designed to track VIX short-term futures by providing a daily rolling long position in the first and second month VIX futures contracts.
- **iPath S&P 500 VIX Mid-Term Futures ETN (VXZ)**: Designed to track VIX mid-term futures by providing a daily rolling long position in the fourth, fifth, sixth, and seventh month VIX futures contracts.

Investors can use these ETNs to create hedges or standalone investments. Furthermore, differences between long- and short-term views of the market often suggest a variety of complex strategies. It might make sense, for example, to short near-term volatility while being long the mid-term. If the market becomes unstable, interest rates rise, or an ongoing rally sputters, those dynamics are likely to be more heavily represented in VXZ than in VXX.

Volatility ETNs also have listed options. These options are relatively expensive. At the time of this writing, VXX was priced at $25, and $25 strike price calls with one month remaining before expiration were trading for $1.70 (60% implied volatility). Selling covered calls, therefore, nets $1.70 per month or $20.40 per year. An investor would simply purchase the VXX and sell at-the-money options each month. Choosing the strike price closest to the trading price of the fund maximizes the amount of time decay priced into the option. This strategy of using monthly sequential option sales to generate income has a very favorable risk profile for a financial instrument like VXX that has a clearly defined lower limit. The reason is simple: Market volatility can never go away, and no force can cause the VIX to crash. Moreover, the kinds of surprises that often rock financial markets normally cause the VIX, and therefore the volatility ETNs, to rise. An investor who pursues the covered call strategy can reasonably expect to own VXX for almost nothing within one year. If, for example, the index remained stable and VXX hovered around $25, the sequential covered call strategy would lower the net acquisition cost to less than $5 within 12 months. Few stocks, if any, present such favorable dynamics for selling covered calls.

Endnotes

1. Feller, W. 1950. *An Introduction to Probability Theory and Its Applications*. New York: Wiley.
2. The CBOE VIX microsite contains historical information, white papers, and links to additional information: http://www.cboe.com/micro/vix/.
3. CBOE calculates several other volatility indexes that complement the VIX. They include the Nasdaq-100 Volatility Index (VXNSM), CBOE DJIA Volatility Index (VXDSM), CBOE Russell 2000 Volatility Index (RVXSM) and CBOE S&P 500 3-Month Volatility Index (VXVSM). In 2008, CBOE pioneered the use of the VIX methodology to estimate the expected volatility of certain commodities and foreign currencies. Included are the CBOE Crude Oil Volatility Index (OVXSM), CBOE Gold Volatility Index (GVZSM), and CBOE EuroCurrency Volatility Index.
4. The iPath site has detailed information about exchange traded notes: www.ipathetn.com.

Chapter 7

Strategies for a New Market

The Most Common Mistake

Investors often make the mistake of assuming that they have unique insights that the market has failed to recognize. They buy stocks that they believe are underpriced, or they purchase high-yielding corporate bonds because their instincts tell them that the risk of default is exaggerated. In the worst cases, these mistakes evolve into an investment strategy.

Unfortunately, the investment community tends to overuse the words "underpriced" and "overpriced." Strictly speaking, a financial instrument cannot be underpriced unless the market is inefficient. The opposite is generally true; markets tend to be very efficient, especially with regard to the pricing of heavily traded stocks that are closely followed by large institutions. An investor who believes he has discovered a discount would usually be better off assuming that he has missed something. Humbleness is the most valuable attribute an investor can have.

Most investors would prefer to believe that they can outthink the market. They continue to believe they have this capability even when they are wrong and lose money. When someone buys a stock and the price falls, they often blame the market or the lack of knowledge of other investors. In modern times it has also become fashionable to blame large institutions and hedge funds. Message boards and investor chat rooms on the internet are filled with various forms of the statement: "Large institutions are driving down the price so they can buy more."

However, when a stock rises, the same person will automatically credit themselves with making a good investment. If the stock rises immediately, they are also likely to take credit for perfect timing. Few investors ever adopt the opposing view that when they make money it's because they are lucky, and when they lose money it's because they made a bad investment decision.

An excellent illustration of this point occurred just a few weeks before this chapter was written in August 2010. The specific event was Amazon's second quarter earnings report. On July 22, 2010, Amazon closed at $120.07. Just a few minutes later, the company announced disappointing second quarter earnings. Analysts had forecasted the company would earn $0.54 per share and the actual number came in at $0.45 per share. The stock plunged in after-hours trading falling $10 in the first minute following the announcement, and another $10 over the next 30 minutes. It then began to stabilize and rallied back to end the after-hours session down $13 at $107. The next morning when the market opened, the plunge continued with the stock opening at $105.93.

But something surprising happened just a few moments after the open—the stock began rising steadily.

The trend continued all day, and when the closing bell rang Amazon was trading at $118.88. Excluding the activities of the overnight session, the stock fell 12% and climbed back 19%, all in the same day.

These changes are even more shocking when they are expressed in option trading terms. Using Amazon's at-the-money option implied volatility of 30%, we can calculate a value of $2.27 for a 1 day, 1 standard deviation price change. The stock, therefore, fell and then immediately recovered more than 5 standard deviations. Option pricing theory predicts that a 5 standard deviation change will occur just once in 1.7 million days—essentially never. The stock continued trading between $115 and $120 for several days before suddenly rising sharply to close above $128 on August 4th.

The wild confusion was caused by a mixture of factors that were difficult for the market to interpret. As just mentioned, the report constituted an earnings miss. However, revenue grew 41% exceeding most expectations. Although exceptional, the revenue growth was tainted by accounting changes that enhanced the year-over-year comparison. This kind of financial engineering often creates turmoil and confusion as analysts attempt to back out the changes so they can make accurate comparisons. Fulfillment costs also jumped 42% and marketing expenses were up 64%. In short the company was expanding, but funding this expansion was an expensive proposition. It was also facing stiff competition in the electronic book distribution market from a variety of competitors including Apple and Google. Finally, with a price earnings ratio approaching 50, many investors considered the stock overpriced.

Nobody really knew if the earnings report was good or bad, and the company's web-based conference call did little to shed light on the situation. It is clear that the earnings miss drove the stock down to $106, but it is definitely not clear what force drove it back up. Even less understandable is the sudden rally to nearly $130 that began a week later on 8/2. Figure 7.1 traces the price of Amazon from the open on 7/19 to the close on 8/6 using 1-minute intervals.

FIGURE 7.1 *Amazon (ticker: AMZN) 7/19/2010 to 8/6/2010 in 1-minute intervals. Dates appear on the x-axis, price on the y-axis.*

The chart contains several unusual features. Most obvious is the large downward price spike that occurred at the market open on 7/23. Next is the rally that recovered $4 of the loss in the first 15 minutes and another $8 by the end of the trading day. Over the next 5 days the stock experienced several large oscillations between

$115 and $120. During these 5 days it experienced several sharp opening declines and immediate rallies back to its closing price of the previous day. Suddenly, however, on 8/2 the stock began rising steadily. At the close it traded above the pre-announcement high of $120. This price became a floor, and the stock rallied sharply for the next 2 days, finally reaching a high above $128.

Figure 7.1 tends to compress much of the wild behavior because it spans a large price range and a small time frame. Most significant were the large fluctuations that occurred between 7/26 and 8/2. These changes are better visualized on the expanded scale of Figure 7.2, which covers the first 5 days after the announcement.

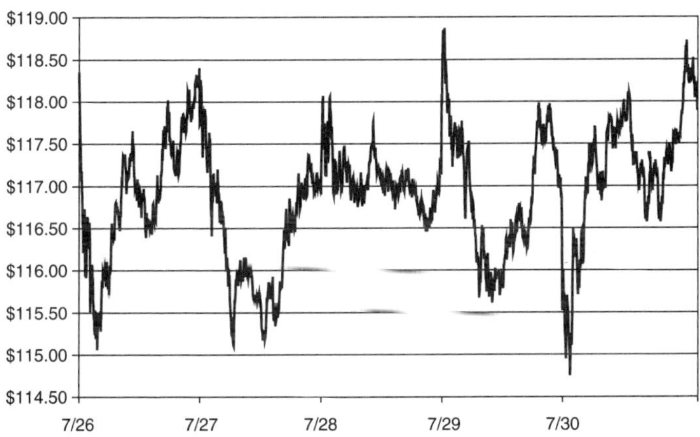

FIGURE 7.2 *Amazon (ticker: AMZN) 7/26/2010–7/30/2010 in 1-minute intervals. Dates appear on the x-axis, price on the y-axis.*

The up and down transitions visible in the chart are completely uncharacteristic for a stock like Amazon with historical and option implied volatility of 30%. In option pricing terms, the stock was rising and falling approximately 2 standard deviations each day. Changes of this magnitude normally occur 5% of the time or once every 20 days. Amazon stock was oscillating at 40 times this frequency.

Each day was also characterized by high volume. On the day of the collapse, 42.4 million shares traded. The next day, volume dropped to 11.1 million—still extremely high. For the remainder of the time frame of our discussion, volume averaged 6.3 million shares per day. Volume information is important because stocks are often manipulated by large institutional investors when trading volume is light. This certainly was not the case for Amazon because, on the day of the sharp decline, more than $5 billion of stock changed hands.

Trying to explain such behavior and make predictions is one of the largest mistakes an investor can make. It is always easy to craft scenarios. For Amazon we might theorize that the large earnings miss was forecasted by a group of investors who maintained short position. When the stock fell $14, these investors began buying to capture profit. This activity caused the stock to rise and forced other short investors to also cover their positions. This kind of "short covering" rally happens all the time, but when it ends the stock normally falls back below its previous low. Amazon displayed none of this behavior so we would have to explain the continued rally back to $118 on 7/23.

New news is usually the cause. In the case of Amazon that news would have come from the earnings conference call. Unfortunately, the call was widely criticized by the analyst community for lack of transparency. Most were angry because they felt the company had misled them by making it difficult to forecast earnings. The large miss hurt their credibility. None of these dynamics favor a rally; they certainly don't explain an unprecedented rally after a sharp decline.

Other minor news items surfaced over the next few weeks. For example, on 8/2 news surfaced that Amazon's new Kindle electronic reader (eReader) was sold out. However, since Amazon gave no information about the size of the backlog or the number it expected to sell, the phrase "sold out" had little real meaning. This information alone could not have triggered a $10 rally of the stock from $118 to $128.

A second related piece of news surfaced after the market closed on 8/3. Shares of competing bookseller Barnes & Noble (ticker: BKS) surged 24.7% to $15.11 after the company said its board of directors was evaluating various strategic alternatives, including a possible sale of the company. In an after-hours press release, the company said its board made the decision because it believed the stock was "significantly undervalued." Barnes & Noble stock had lost more than half its value over the previous 8 months with Amazon as its major competitor. The two companies had completely different business models. One view, therefore, was that uncertainty about the future of Barnes & Noble was likely to cause money to flow out of its stock and into Amazon's. Another was that the demise of BKS represented a validation of Amazon's business model. Many investors try to capitalize on such situations by trading the two stocks against each other. They purchase the stronger stock and short the weaker one. If the market rallies, they expect the strong stock to outperform the weak one, and the long position to gain more than the short side loses. Conversely if the market declines, they expect to realize a larger gain from the short position than their loss on the long side. This approach caused some investors to buy AMZN and sell short BKS with the view that AMZN would outperform BKS on "up" days and BKS will fall more sharply on "down" days. This trade would have been profitable after the Barnes & Noble announcement because the stock fell 6.7% over the next 3 days while AMZN climbed 4%.

This approach to trading stocks against each other should not be confused with traditional "pairs" trading—a statistical approach that involves identifying two stocks that tend to move together and taking advantage of a break in the correlation by shorting the rising stock and buying its falling counterpart. When the correlation resumes and their behavior realigns, both sides of the trade can be closed for a profit. This strategy is the exact inverse of buying the strong stock and selling the weak one. The first approach is usually intended as a long-term strategy while the statistical pairs trade might only last for a few minutes. Both types of trades are common in situations like the one involving Amazon and Barnes & Noble. The companies are competitors with distinctly different business models, and both stocks were affected by significant news announcements during the same week.

The remainder of the story had not played out when these words were written. The concepts, however, are helpful for illustrating key points in our discussion. The

Amazon earnings story was chosen to help illustrate the fallacy involved in making predictions about the direction of a stock. No technical chart could have predicted the earnings miss, and stock analysts who closely follow the company were caught completely off guard. The market responded, as might be expected, by aggressively selling the stock. That behavior ended almost immediately, and nobody has offered a reasonable explanation for the sharp rally that followed the violent sell off. Such an explanation would need to take into account the complex dynamics of algorithmic trading (including pairs trading), rising and falling short interest in both stocks, behavior of the broad market, reactions to news, and rumors circulating between institutional investors.

Both long and short investors had many opportunities to generate substantial profits. Those who were short before the earnings announcement would have maximized their profits by closing their trades in the after-hours session that followed. Most, however, waited until the market opened the following morning. That approach also generated a very substantial return. Conversely, anyone who purchased the stock after the downward price spike ultimately generated a very large profit by the end of the trading day because the stock climbed more than $12 from its opening low.

Figure 7.2 reveals a surprising number of opportunities for active traders. The highly volatile time frame depicted in the chart contains approximately $26 worth of up and down price transitions. Investors who found themselves on the winning side of one or several of these trades probably believed that their profits resulted from proper timing and trade execution. Those who lost money were likely frustrated by the erratic behavior of the stock. As always, many traders who lost money ultimately determined that the behavior of the entire market caused confusion by affecting the price of the stock in unpredictable ways. This interpretation was partly correct because the broad market also experienced several large transitions during this time frame.

A more accurate view would be that some individuals were lucky and others were not. Many knowledgeable investors who carefully planned their trades lost money while others who correctly guessed the direction got lucky. Some who owned the stock simply held on through the collapse because they believed the market was wrong. Others panicked out only to discover a few hours later that their original position would have been profitable. One dynamic is clear—being lucky is better than being smart.

Finally, many investors reading these words will declare that short-term trading is always difficult because precisely timing the market is impossible. They believe, however, that they have a better chance of making accurate long-term predictions. That belief implies that complexity and uncertainty decrease over time. Unfortunately the opposite is true—complexity and uncertainty tend to increase as new forces come into play. The Amazon earnings story highlights this problem. Complex as the situation might appear, it can't compare to the uncertainty of the future, which includes new competitors, new products, and an ever-changing marketplace. Nothing changes faster than the future.

The options market understands that uncertainty increases over time. It typically responds by increasing the implied volatility of far-dated contracts. When this chapter was written, Amazon current month options were priced with 30% implied volatility while long-term options expiring in 18 months were priced at 36%.

A Few Simple Dynamics

Stocks rise when buyers are more aggressive than sellers. They fall when sellers are more aggressive than buyers. Most investors mistakenly believe that stocks rise when there are more buyers than sellers. The difference is significant and it has far-reaching implications. Liquid markets always have an excess of both buyers and sellers who generate bid and ask prices. A transaction occurs when the high bid and low ask come together; either the bid is raised or the ask is lowered. A rising bid represents aggressive buying and a falling ask represents aggressive selling. Aggressive buying drives up the transaction price while aggressive selling lowers it.

Buyers and sellers can become aggressive for many different reasons. Triggers can include news about the economy, other stocks, or individual industries. Money can also flow in or out of other markets as interest rates rise and fall and currency exchange rates fluctuate. News surprises also cause investors to shift money between stocks in the same sector. This dynamic was mentioned above as a possible cause of the sharp rise in Amazon's share price after Barnes & Noble announced that its board of directors was contemplating a sale of the company.

Extending this analysis reveals that investment vehicles constantly compete with each other. The nature of the competition is always changing. Money can flow from one market to another (bonds versus stocks); from one sector to another (high tech versus manufacturing); from one from one area of the world to another (mature versus emerging market); or between stocks in the same sector (Pfizer versus Merck). Investors make these choices thousands of times each day. Simply stated, money that flows into the stock market does not flow evenly into all stocks. As mentioned in the previous section, these dynamics are often used to create hedges that offset a long investment in one stock against a short position in another.

It is also important to understand the underlying forces that cause investors to become aggressive buyers or sellers of a stock or other financial instrument. The dynamics are simple. At any given time, the market sets a price that comprehends everything that can be known about a particular stock including confidential information known only to insiders. The moment new information becomes available, market forces adjust the price.

Every stock trades at a characteristic price/earnings (PE) ratio. The market bids up the price of a stock when it anticipates that earnings will rise sharply. A high PE, therefore, is the market's way of predicting future growth and pricing that growth into a stock. Analysts raise their "price target" for a particular stock, when their forward-looking view reveals that earnings will rise faster than previously forecast. If the market completely agreed with the new forecast, the price would immediately rise to equal the new predicted value. The difference between a stock's trading price and an analyst's future price target is important because it represents the difference between two views. The market votes with real money and analysts vote with words on paper. Sometimes the gap reverses because information surfaces that causes the market to become more bullish on a stock than existing forecasts. The more optimistic view will drive the price above targets already set by the analyst community. If the situation persists, analysts will raise their forecasts.

Unfortunately, investors often misinterpret the meaning of price targets set by the analyst community. The common belief is that stocks experience steady growth, and that they are always are on a trajectory to reach a future target. In reality, there is no trajectory. The price will remain flat if a company continues to perform as predicted by the market. IBM's performance during the first half of 2010 is a perfect example of this phenomenon. The price hovered in the $120s from November 2009 through July 2010 despite three quarterly reports that revealed steadily rising earnings. Rising earnings measured against a flat stock price resulted in a declining PE. The analyst community, however, maintained year-end price targets around $150. The gap between analysts' expectations and the actual trading price resulted from the market's view, not a trajectory for the stock. Many investors who misinterpreted this difference believed that the stock was "underpriced." Their views were partly based on elevated price targets and a surprisingly low PE compared to the rest of the industry. These views were often expressed in articles, forecasts, blogs, and web-based chat rooms.

There is certainly nothing wrong with having a different view than the market; insightful investors who understand and closely follow a company may well be able to outperform the crowd. But it is important for these investors to understand how their views differ from that of the collective market. In the case of IBM, the market's discounted PE represented a collective view that earnings growth—for whatever reason—would not be sustained. With each quarter's report, earnings rose, the stock fluctuated around the same price, and the PE fell. Bullish investors expected the price, and consequently the PE, to rise because they believed that the market was missing something. Bearish investors believed that earnings were rising for the wrong reasons. Their list generally included cost-cutting measures such as layoffs, currency exchange rate adjustments, tax model changes, stock buy backs that reduced the number of outstanding shares, and low interest rate borrowing. Because such activities cannot be sustained forever, these investors believed that earnings growth would not be sustained. Lack of revenue growth was their most important indicator. For the most part, the analyst community believed that the company would deliver both earnings and revenue growth. The market's view was somewhere in the middle.

It is also important to recognize that analyst predictions can be dramatically wrong if new information surfaces. On January 4, 2010—the first trading day of the year—Google traded above $620. Several analysts set year-end price targets above $800 because they believed the market had underpriced the stock. They were dead wrong. Six months later on July 1st, the stock closed at

$439. During that time frame, the company reported both outstanding earnings and revenue growth. Most dramatic was the behavior following the first quarter report after the market closed on 4/15. The numbers were nothing short of spectacular. The company earned $6.06 per share (nearly $2 billion), an increase of more than 37% from the same quarter in the previous year. Revenue climbed 23% to $6.78 billion establishing Google's strongest growth since the third quarter of 2008. Surprisingly, the stock immediately fell $45 to close at $550.15. The trend continued, taking another $110 off the price by July 1st.

The important question is why? Immediately after the earnings were reported, while the stock was falling, analysts reaffirmed a forecast of 20% revenue growth through the end of the year. Bullish investors, many who traded for large institutional accounts, were crushed by the surprise. The problem was rooted in uncertainty. The brightening outlook was encouraging Google to spend more money and expand into new markets. The company's discussion revealed a strategy that included acquisitions, new hiring, and aggressive expansion into the intelligent mobile phone market. Eric Schmidt, Google's chief executive, told investors that the company will likely make at least one acquisition per month, "some big, more small." The company's biggest pending acquisition was a proposed agreement to buy AdMob, a mobile advertising service, for $750 million.

Investors were worried about those commitments because Google would not say how much it was prepared to spend, and over what length of time. The discussion raised worries that the company's profit margins might not expand as rapidly as its revenue. These dynamics reveal the sensitivity that normally develops around overly bullish forecasts. When a stock rallies for a long period of time, continually exceeding both analysts' forecasts and the market's expectations, the performance bar that the company must jump over can rise impossibly high. As previously stated, there is no price trajectory; the current price of a stock simply reflects the markets collective forward looking view. When that view changes, so does the price. In the case of Google, the forward looking view became less certain, and the market rapidly applied a discount to the numbers. Bears won and bulls lost, not because their analysis was better, but because new information became available. Nobody could have forecasted that Google would announce a number of expensive initiatives, and that the market would be dissatisfied with the level of financial detail. Moreover, nobody could reasonably have anticipated that shattering analysts' expectations for both top line revenue growth and earnings would result in a 5.2 standard deviation decline—the magnitude as measured in option trading terms.

Diversification Versus Hedging

Buying stocks is a dangerous way to invest. On any given day, for a variety of impossible-to-forecast reasons, the price of a stock can plunge destroying billions of dollars of value. The one-day drop in Google mentioned above cost investors more than $12 billion dollars. Such stories highlight the need for a better approach to investing.

Most investors would be surprised to learn that stock investments are also dangerous from a purely technical perspective. Money managers and stock brokers tend to solve the problem by telling their clients to "diversify." The word has taken on an oddly positive connotation. In reality, it signals a lack of commitment and an acknowledgment that the future is uncertain. Investors who diversify tend to view each addition to their portfolio as a new chance to win. A more accurate view would be that each new position represents both a chance to win and a chance to lose. Those who recognize that increased opportunity is always paired with additional risk, tend to fall back on diversification as a way to spread the risk around while increasing their chance of success. It's the exact same approach that gamblers use when they place multiple bets. Unfortunately, diversification is an overly simplistic and ineffective way to hedge. More effective solutions involve structured positions that use both options and stock, or just options alone.

The sections that follow review some basic alternatives to owning stock. The discussions are intended as an introduction; each topic by itself could serve as the subject of an entire book. In each case, we review an alternative trade that is both less expensive and safer than a simple stock position. We also review the concept of using options to create "synthetic" stock. Taken together, these concepts should prove valuable to any investor who wishes to manage risk by limiting market exposure. We begin with the most conservative stock/option hybrid: a collar.

Collars

The simplest way to protect a stock position is by purchasing a put. If the stock declines, the value of the put will rise to offset the loss. Both the level of protection and the cost are determined by the strike price. Far out-of-the-money puts provide less protection; near-the-money puts provide more. The least expensive and least protective options are both far-dated and far out-of-the-money. Investors who purchase such options usually consider them as "disaster" insurance.

For most investors, it makes sense to cap losses relatively close to the current trading price of a stock. As the price changes, it makes sense to move up the strike price of the put. These dynamics dictate that the option should be both near-the-money and close to expiration. Each time the option expires, a new hedge can be placed at the most appropriate price.

Purchasing new puts each month is an expensive proposition that is likely to consume a large amount of profit. Fortunately there is a better way. The answer is to pay for each month's long put by selling a similarly-priced out-of-the-money call. The complete position is called a collar.

A collar limits the maximum loss of a position in exchange for a cap on the potential gain. The maximum loss is determined by the strike price of the long put; the gain is capped at the strike price of the short call. The option portion of the collar normally costs nothing because the long put is paid for by selling the call. A new collar can be constructed each month using options that symmetrically bracket the stock price. Table 7.1

displays an example of a collar on the SPDR Gold Trust (ticker: GLD)—a popular exchange traded fund (ETF). The example was structured using stock and option prices at the close on 8/9/2010.

TABLE 7.1 *Collar Trade Example Using SPDR Gold Trust Prices on 8/9/2010.*

Description	Position on 8/9/2010	Price($)	Position($)
GLD	Long 100 shares	117.40	11,740.00
$122 call	Short 1 contract (expires 9/17)	0.86	(86.00)
$112 put	Long 1 contract (expires 9/17)	0.75	75.00

The option contracts used to structure the collar had 39 days remaining before expiration. This particular example is nearly symmetrical with both put and call strikes $5 away from the trading price of the stock. If the stock closes above $122 when the options expire on September 17, the trade will generate a $4.60 profit. The gain is limited at the upper strike ($122), because above this price there is a cost associated with buying back the short calls. This expense rises point-for-point with the value of the stock above $122. Conversely, the calls will expire worthless if the stock closes below $122 on September 17.

The maximum loss, no matter how far the stock falls, is limited to $5.40—the distance to the long put. Beyond this point, the value of the long put will rise by an amount exactly equal to the loss in the stock. For example, if the stock collapses to $90, the $112 put will be worth $22, which will offset all but $5.40 of the $27.40 stock loss. Table 7.2 summarizes the net value of the trade for various stock prices at options expiration.

TABLE 7.2 *Summary Results at Various Possible Closing Prices for GLD Collar on September 17*

Description	Position on 8/9/2010	Initial($)	Final($)	Net($)	Trade($)
GLD	Long 100 shares	117.40	90.00	(27.40)	
$122 call	Short 1 contract	0.86	0.00	0.86	
$112 put	Long 1 contract	0.75	22.00	21.25	(5.29)
GLD	Long 100 shares	117.40	130.00	12.60	
$122 call	Short 1 contract	0.86	8.00	(7.14)	
$112 put	Long 1 contract	0.75	0.00	(0.75)	4.71
GLD	Long 100 shares	117.40	122.00	4.60	
$122 call	Short 1 contract	0.86	0.00	0.86	
$112 put	Long 1 contract	0.75	0.00	(0.75)	4.71
GLD	Long 100 shares	117.40	121.00	3.60	
$122 call	Short 1 contract	0.86	0.00	0.86	
$112 put	Long 1 contract	0.75	0.00	(0.75)	3.71

The table is divided into four sections: sharp decline to $90, strong rally to $130, rise to the upper strike ($122), rise to $1 below the upper strike ($121). Each reveals important details about the trade.

In the first scenario where the stock falls sharply to $90, the loss is capped by the rise in value of the long put. For each $1 of stock value lost below $112, the put gains $1. Because the strike price of the put is $112, its value at expiration is $22. The results presented in the table also take into account the slight difference in price between the short call and the long put. Each trade, therefore, generates an extra $0.11. The net loss, which would have been $27.40, is capped at only $5.29 ($2,740 versus $529 for 100 shares).

The second scenario describes the behavior of the trade following a strong rally to $130. In this case, the long put expires worthless but the short call must be repurchased to close the trade. Once the strike price is crossed, the cost of repurchasing the call rises $1 for each $1 gain in the stock. The net gain, therefore, is capped at $4.71 ($471 for 100 shares) which is equal to the stock increase from $117.40 to the call strike ($122) plus the additional $0.11 mentioned previously.

The third scenario delivers the same result as the second. It was included to demonstrate that maximum profit is achieved if the stock rises to strike price of the short call. At this exact price, all the stock gain is kept as profit, and both options expire worthless.

The fourth scenario is similar to the third in the sense that both options are simply left to expire. However, the stock gain is $1 smaller, so the net trade delivers $3.71 ($371 for 100 shares). As before, the precise net gain includes the $0.11 difference in the initial option prices.

The trade can be repeated each month by bracketing the stock at its new price with another pair of long and short options. In each case, the investor is free to decide how much risk to take and where to cap the maximum gain. If, for example, the outlook is extremely bullish, the strike prices might be placed far apart. They can also be spaced asymmetrically, most often with the put side narrower than the call side. This approach makes the trade more expensive as the short call will not cover the entire cost of the long put. However, the more expensive trade is also worth more because it has lower risk. Finally, symmetrical spacing at no cost can be difficult to achieve when the implied volatility skew causes out-of-the-money puts to be priced higher than equivalently far out-of-the-money calls. Most option traders choose strikes that are similarly priced, which causes the put side spacing to be slightly wider than the call side. Table 7.3 illustrates this phenomenon using next-month options on Amazon.com stock as they were priced at the close on 8/10/2010 with the stock at exactly $130.00.

TABLE 7.3 *Pricing Details for Symmetrically Spaced Put and Call Options on Amazon.com at the Close on 8/10/2010 (The final trading price for the stock was exactly $130.00. The options were set to expire in 38 days.)*

Option	Bid($)	Ask($)	Mid($)	Implied Vol.	Difference
$130 call	5.45	5.55	5.50	32.1%	
$130 put	5.55	5.65	5.60	33.4%	1.8%
$135 call	3.15	3.30	3.23	30.7%	
$125 put	3.60	3.65	3.63	35.1%	12.4%
$140 call	1.70	1.75	1.73	29.8%	
$120 put	2.31	2.36	2.34	37.5%	35.4%
$145 call	0.82	0.87	0.85	29.3%	
$115 put	1.47	1.52	1.50	40.2%	76.9%
$150 call	0.36	0.41	0.39	28.9%	
$110 put	0.94	0.97	0.96	43.1%	148.1%

Amazon.com was chosen for this example because the stock's closing price on 8/10/2010 provided a unique opportunity to compare the prices of put and call options with strikes that were precisely the same distance from the closing price of the stock. Each set of entries in the table displays a different symmetrical pair. Columns 2 to 4 provide bid, ask, and midpoint prices. Implied volatility (column 5) is calculated at the midpoint. The price difference (column 6) is calculated as the increased cost of the put over the call.

Column 6 reveals that put and call prices diverge rapidly as the distance to the strikes increases. The difference is insignificant for the first pair of entries in the table because put:call parity causes options at the same strike to be identically priced.[1] However, an investor who structures a wide collar using $20 out-of-the-money options would pay $0.96 for the protective long put position and only $0.39 of the cost would be defrayed by the sale of a symmetrical call. The steep skew is evident in implied volatility values for the two options—43.1% for the put and only 28.9% for the call.

Many different strike price and date combinations are available for heavily traded stocks. In many cases, weekly options provide the opportunity to adjust the bracket more frequently. This fine control is helpful when market conditions change, or a stock moves sharply in response to news.

Collars top the list of conservative trades and, in most cases, they outperform simple long stock positions. Stock investors who structure positions without options must use stop orders to protect themselves. This approach has many drawbacks, most notably the effect of being forced out of a trade that later becomes profitable. A stock/option trade can always be structured to limit the maximum loss at any desired level. However, because the option position need not be closed before expiration, a losing trade that has realized its maximum loss can be kept open with the hope that the stock will rally back into a range where the trade is profitable. Stock investors who regret being stopped out sometimes reopen the same trade only to realize additional losses when the stock continues falling. In the worst case they suffer repeated losses trying to find the bottom of a downtrend. Option traders who understand how difficult it can be to spot the bottom of a trend can simply leave their trade alone and wait for a rally.

The next section discusses another hedged structure that is also safer and delivers a much stronger profit than a simple long stock position. This particular structure, although bullish, can deliver a strong profit even if the stock continues to decline at a modest rate.

Vertical Bull Spreads

Most investors don't realize that simple stock positions are inherently risky. They are also much more expensive than equivalent structures that can be created with options. The majority of option traders never buy a stock because they have more sophisticated ways to accomplish the exact same goal.

An option trader with a bullish view on a stock might, for example, sell an out-of-the-money put and hedge with a put at a lower strike price. This type of vertical spread has a maximum loss that is set by the distance between the strikes, and a maximum gain equal to the credit of the trade. We can construct a simple example using the information already presented in Table 7.3. Assuming that we have a bullish view of Amazon, we might sell the $125 put for $3.63 and purchase the $115 put for $1.50. The net credit of this trade would be $2.13.

The full credit of the trade will be retained as profit as long as the stock doesn't fall more than $5 during the month that remains before expiration. If we are wrong and the stock falls more than $15, our loss will be capped by the distance between the strikes. With the stock trading below $115 at expiration, the $125 put will be worth $10 more than the $115 put, and the trade will lose this amount minus the original credit ($10.00 – $2.13 = $7.87).

Suppose, for example, that Amazon falls all the way to $100. We would need to buy back the $125 short put for $25, and our long $115 put would be worth $15. Since our trade had an initial credit of $2.13, the total loss would be equal to the difference ($10) minus the original credit ($2.13), which we would still keep. The trade cannot lose more than this amount no matter how far the stock falls.

Unlike a long stock position, which always loses money if the price declines, this trade generates a profit as long as the stock remains above the price of the short put. We would still keep our initial $2.13 credit if Amazon fell from $130 to $125 over the remaining month. However, we cannot make more than $2.13 no matter how high the stock rises. As with a collar, the maximum gain and loss for the month are both capped. If we repeated this trade each month, and the stock continued to rally without any setbacks larger than $5, our trades would generate more than $25 over the span of a single year. A bullish trader would, therefore, be able to generate a 19% annual return even if the stock declined $5 each month.

It is also important to recognize that purchasing a vertical spread is far less expensive than purchasing stock. The collateral requirement for this trade is based on the maximum loss, which is equal to the $10 space between the strike prices. The account would, therefore, need to have at least $1,000 to cover each contract—a small amount compared to the $13,000 that would be required to purchase 100 shares of stock at $130. This simple option trade would, therefore, generate a 250% return over the time frame of a single year, even if the stock declined at a steady rate of $5 per month.

In summary, a vertical bull spread is many times less expensive, considerably safer, and almost always more profitable than an ordinary long stock position.

Covered Calls

A short call is considered covered if the account also contains an opposing market position composed of an equivalent amount of stock. An example would be the sale of 1 call contract in an account that also contains 100 shares of the underlying stock.[2]

There are a variety of reasons for selling calls against a long stock position. Over time, the revenue from calls tends to add up to a value that represents a significant discount of the stock price. For this reason, covered call strategies almost always outperform simple stock ownership. Long stock positions only outperform covered call strategies in unusual circumstances where a stock rises substantially for an extended period of time. When the rally finally ends, however, the covered call strategy will quickly catch up. Investors who consistently sell calls against their stock positions have more stable portfolios that deliver more constant returns.

The IBM story outlined earlier in this chapter serves an excellent illustration of the power of covered call writing. Shareholders were frustrated as the stock drifted up and down between $120 and $130 from

November 2009 through July 2010. However, an investor who repeatedly sold covered calls using at-the-money options would have generated more than $3 of revenue each month. This approach generated more than $30 of profit during the 10 months that the stock stood still. The trade was safer and much more profitable than simply owning the stock. Its only assumption was that the stock would not decline sharply, but even modest declines would have been absorbed by the cumulative value of sequential option sales. Over the course of an entire year, the trade would have been protected against a decline of more than 25% in the underlying stock. In this regard it is also important to note that when a stock declines, implied volatility rises driving up the price of the options. If the stock declines rapidly, most covered call writers will buy back their short position and sell new calls at a lower strike price. This approach can easily double or triple the revenue collected during a single month. The covered call strategy will always fill the gap unless the stock continues to fall for an extended period of time.

Covered call strategies vary considerably. The most bullish investors tend to sell inexpensive out-of-the-money options because they expect the stock to rise in the short term, and they prefer not to cap their maximum gain with a low strike price. Less bullish and slightly bearish investors often sell expensive at-the-money options. Their goal is to profit from the option premium while using the stock as a hedge against the short call position.

Back testing the covered call strategy for IBM gives surprisingly strong results over long periods of time. If, for example, we began selling monthly at-the-money options in January 2007, the strategy would have generated more than $80 of profit over 36 months: $8,000 for 100 shares of stock. In each case, we would have sold calls at the closest strike just above the trading price on expiration day and closed the trade at the next expiration. The stock began the time frame of our test trading around $100, climbed as high as $130 in July 2008, fell below $70 in November of the same year, and rallied back to $130 in January 2010. A long-term stock investor who held on through the rallies and sell-offs would ultimately have realized a gain of only $30.

Options expired in-the-money 18 of 36 months. The average cost of repurchasing these options was $4.47 or $2.24 more than the average premium received. An alternative approach is to simply allow the stock to be called away, keep the option premium, and immediately replace the position with a new covered trade. A long-term investor who began this process 5 years ago would now own IBM stock for free: an incredible gain considering that the stock traded for the same price in July 2010 as it did 10 years earlier in July 2000.

Weekly Options—An Unprecedented Opportunity

The availability of weekly options on many stocks has made this approach even more attractive. For example, at the time of this writing, weekly options on Apple Computer averaged $3.41 of pure time premium with sequential weekly sales yielding a staggering $177 on an annual basis. With the stock trading at $250, an investor who repeats this sale each week can expect to own the stock for free in 74 weeks.[3] Moreover, the trade will be profitable unless Apple declines more than $177 over the next 12 months.

The phrase "pure time premium" was carefully chosen because the calculation includes both in and out-of-the-money options. The time value realized from an option sale is greatest when the stock trades at the strike price of the option. The most accurate calculation of the weekly average must, therefore, assume that the stock will trade anywhere from $5 below the strike to $5 above the strike each time a new call is sold. Additionally, since our goal is to sell time premium—the portion of the option price that decays as expiration approaches—we must discount in-the-money options by the distance above the strike price. For example, if a $100 call on a $102 stock trades for $5, then the price includes $3 of time premium ($2 for the amount that the stock is in-the-money and another $3 of time value). The $3.41 average weekly call price reflects all of these factors and includes only the time premium portion of in-the-money options.

This opportunity is extraordinary but completely realistic. It makes perfect sense for options to be priced this way because $3.41 represents a relatively small price change for Apple. (A 1-day, 1-standard deviation change was equal to $5.05 when this chapter was written.) The distortion, in part, is due to the overlap between Thursday morning when the next week's option appears, and Friday afternoon when the previous week's option expires. This overlap yields 1.27 additional days of decay each week or 66 days each year.

The price dynamics outlined for the Apple trade are actually better than the numbers suggest because the value of at-the-money options would increase substantially as the stock climbed—at-the-money weekly options would be worth $9.13 with the stock trading at $400. If the bullish view were wrong and the stock fell sharply, implied volatility would increase, keeping the premium level artificially high. Option traders who understand these dynamics frequently use them to model new trades.

Selling At-the-Money Puts

Most investors would be surprised to learn that selling an at-the-money put is mathematically identical to selling an at-the-money covered call. Both trades are safer than simple stock ownership; both deliver better profits. An investor who purchases a stock for long-term ownership would do much better to simply sell an at-the-money put. As before, repeating the trade each month is preferable because it maximizes the net time decay. The difference between short and long-term options is enormous. For example, when these words were written, Research in Motion (ticker: RIMM) $50 puts with 36 days remaining before expiration traded for $1.72. (The stock traded at $54.) The equivalent long-term option with 526 days remaining traded for $8.80. Although it had nearly 15 times as many days left before expiration, the long-dated option traded for only 5 times the price. Applying the 15x multiplier, however, yields a compounded value of $25.80 for sequential sales of near-dated options. Sequential sales generate nearly 3 times the value.

Table 7.4 demonstrates the mathematical equivalence of the two trades by comparing the results of three different scenarios.

TABLE 7.4 *Comparison of Short At-the-Money Put and At-the-Money Covered Call Strategies*

Description	Initial($)	Final($)	Net($)	Trade($)
Scenario 1				
Long stock	100.00	90.00	(10.00)	
Short $100 call	4.00	0.00	4.00	(6.00)
Short $100 put	(4.00)	(10.00)	(6.00)	(6.00)
Scenario 2				
Long stock	100.00	110.00	10.00	
Short $100 call	4.00	10.00	(6.00)	4.00
Short $100 put	(4.00)	0.00	4.00	4.00
Scenario 3				
Long stock	100.00	100.00	0.00	
Short $100 call	4.00	0.00	4.00	4.00
Short $100 put	(4.00)	0.00	4.00	4.00

Each grouping in the table contains two trades. The top two rows describe a covered at-the-money call. The third row, below the space, contains a short at-the-money put trade.

- In scenario 1, the stock falls $10. This loss is partly offset by the $4 premium received from the sale of the call. The trade, therefore, suffers a net loss of $6. The short put trade loses exactly the same amount with the option price rising from its initial $4 to $10. The contracts would need to be repurchased at expiration.

- Scenario 2 reveals the results of a $10 increase in the stock price. This increase is offset by a $6 increase in the value of the short call, which reduces the net gain of the trade to $4. The short put trade yields the exact same return in the form of option premium retained when the contracts expire.
- Scenario 3 involves a flat stock price. Although no money is gained or lost in the stock, both trades gain $4 in the form of option premium.

Although both outcomes are the same, the short put strategy has a distinct price advantage over the covered call approach. The collateral requirement for a "naked" put is equal to 20% of the value of the underlying stock. Since 1 contract represents 100 shares, selling a naked at-the-money put on a $100 stock requires $2,000 ($100 stock x 100 shares x 20%). The equivalent covered call strategy requires that $10,000 be set aside to purchase 100 shares of stock.

Recasting the previously mentioned IBM covered call trade using short puts yields a tremendous return. Whereas the covered call approach required $10,000 for every 100 shares purchased, the short put version would require only $2,200 of collateral for each contract sold. This value is based on the average price of the stock ($108) over the 36 months used for the example. The $8,000 gain, therefore, represents an 80% return for the sequential covered call approach, but a 264% return for the short put strategy.

Each of these strategies can be reversed when appropriate. Bearish investors, for example, might choose to create a covered put position (short stock and short put) or sell at-the-money calls. Markets and individual stocks rise and fall, and it is just as easy to make money in a falling market as in a rising one. Falling markets also present additional opportunities to option traders in the form of higher implied volatility and steeper volatility skews. When the long-term outlook is negative, far-dated options also become more expensive. Each adjustment, distortion, or anomaly represents additional opportunity to option traders who balance stock positions with option trades. During the crash of 2008, for example, some options were priced with volatility in the hundreds of percent, even after the stocks had declined to a fraction of their previous value. Goldman Sachs was an excellent example. In November 2007 the stock traded as high as $250; 1 year later it had fallen to a low of $47 with the options market pricing in another $20 of decline. When the stock finally began to recover, high implied volatility persisted for several months providing option traders with enormous opportunities to sell overpriced options. In this environment it was possible to generate 100% returns in only a couple of months, strictly by selling time premium. These returns would have accrued even if the stock had stagnated.

Synthetic Stock

Our discussion has focused on stock and option trades that are designed to replace traditional long stock positions. Although superior in terms of both risk and average return, none of these trades is mathematically equivalent to owning stock. It is, however, possible to structure synthetic stock positions using only options.

Unlike the option trades described above, these positions do not cap the maximum gain in return for reduced downside risk. They also lack the ability to generate a profit if the stock remains flat or declines slightly. In short, they behave exactly as if they were stock; their only advantage is reduced cost.

The basic trade involves buying at-the-money calls and selling at-the-money puts. The comparison is outlined in Table 7.5.

TABLE 7.5 *Synthetic Versus Real Stock*

Description	Initial($)	Final($)	Net($)	Trade($)
Scenario 1				
Long $100 call	3.50	0.00	(3.50)	
Short $100 put	3.50	10.00	(6.50)	(10.00)
Long stock	100.00	90.00	(10.00)	(10.00)
Scenario 2				
Long $100 call	3.50	10.00	6.50	
Short $100 put	3.50	0.00	3.50	10.00
Long stock	100.00	110.00	10.00	10.00
Scenario 3				
Long $100 call	3.50	0.00	(3.50)	
Short $100 put	3.50	0.00	3.50	0.00
Long stock	100.00	100.00	0.00	0.00

Each grouping in the table contains two trades. The top two rows describe a synthetic stock position composed of a long call and a short put. The third row, below the space, contains a simple long stock position.

- In scenario 1, the stock falls $10. That loss is exactly mirrored in the synthetic stock position where the short put must be repurchased for a net loss of $6.50, and the long call loses its initial value of $3.50.
- In scenario 2, the stock rises $10. The gain is exactly mirrored in the synthetic stock position where the long call gains $6.50, and the short put expires worthless generating a $3.50 profit.
- Scenario 3 involves a flat stock price. No money is gained or lost in the stock, and all options expire worthless yielding a $3.50 gain on the put side that is exactly offset by a $3.50 loss on the call side.

The synthetic and real stock positions yielded identical results in all three scenarios. However, the synthetic position is considerably less expensive because, as before, the only cost is the collateral for the short put side of the trade. As before, the account would need $2,000 for each $100 put contact sold. Purchasing 100 shares of stock would be five times as expensive.

Deep In-the-Money Puts and Calls

The delta of an option is the amount that its price will change when the underlying stock moves $1. Deep in-the-money (DITM) options have a delta that is near or equal to 1; that is, their price moves up and down almost exactly the same amount as the underlying stock. Experienced traders often exploit this property by substituting DITM options for long stock positions. They either sell DITM puts or buy DITM calls. These trades are simple to execute, less expensive, and have properties that make them superior to simple stock ownership.

As we shall see, long call and short put trades have different properties and represent slightly different approaches to creating a bullish investment. The differences are subtle, but significant. A simple example that compares the two approaches for three different outcomes is outlined in Table 7.6. Our goal is to replace the purchase of an expensive stock with either long DITM calls or short DITM puts.

TABLE 7.6 ***Comparison of DITM Long Call and DITM Short Put Trades Constructed with Near-Term Options (35 days)***

Description	Initial($)	Final($)	Net($)
Scenario 1			
Long stock	150.00	120.00	(30.00)
Long $130 call	20.00	0.00	(20.00)
Short $170 put	20.00	50.00	(30.00)
Scenario 2			
Long stock	150.00	180.00	30.00
Long $130 call	20.00	50.00	30.00
Short $170 put	20.00	0.00	20.00
Scenario 3			
Long stock	150.00	165.00	15.00
Long $130 call	20.00	35.00	15.00
Short $170 put	20.00	5.00	15.00

Three outcomes of three different trades—long stock, long call, and short put—are represented. As before, each scenario represents a different outcome.

- In scenario 1, the stock falls $30. That loss is exactly mirrored in the short put position. The long call position outperforms the others because it can never lose more than the initial cost of the trade—in this case $20.

- In scenario 2, the stock rises $30. The gain is exactly mirrored in the long call position. The short puts underperform because their gain is capped by the credit of the initial trade—in this case $20.
- Scenario 3 involves a modest $15 price increase. All three trades perform identically.

This example was constructed using actual trading prices of Goldman Sachs stock and options on 8/13/2010. The options had 35 days remaining before expiration. The long call trade was superior because it limited the downside loss in scenario 1 without capping the upside gain in scenario 2. These differences become important in extreme cases like market crashes and company acquisitions.

Table 7.6 was intentionally constructed using near-term options that lacked additional time premium. The trades are easy to understand because they gain or lose the same amount over a relatively large range of price changes. Results are identical for both approaches as long as the underlying stock rises or falls less than $30 over the month of the trade.

Significant differences appear if we narrow the strike spacing or lengthen the time. Long term investors frequently use these dynamics to profit from both the gain of the stock and time decay of the option. Table 7.7 reveals the advantage that can be gained over the long term by selling DITM in-the-money puts.

TABLE 7.7 *Comparison of DITM Long Call and DITM Short Put Trades Constructed with Long-Term Options (161 Days)*

Description	Initial($)	Final($)	Net($)
Scenario 1			
Long stock	150.00	120.00	(30.00)
Long $130 call	26.85	0.00	(26.85)
Short $170 put	25.70	50.00	(24.30)
Scenario 2			
Long stock	150.00	180.00	30.00
Long $130 call	26.85	50.00	23.15
Short $170 put	25.70	0.00	25.70
Scenario 3			
Long stock	150.00	165.00	15.00
Long $130 call	26.85	35.00	8.15
Short $170 put	25.70	5.00	20.70

As before, the values in the table reflect stock and option prices for Goldman Sachs on 8/13/2010. The time frame, however, was extended with both put and call options expiring in 161 days.

- In scenario 1, the stock falls $30. The short put position loses slightly less because the price of the initial trade included $5.70 of time premium. The investor who took the other side of this trade would only realize a profit if the stock fell below $144.30. The long call position initially had $6.85 of time premium; that value was completely lost. Because time premium in the long call is lost while time premium in the short put is retained, the short put trade has a $12.55 advantage. The two trades, therefore, would lose the same amount of money if the stock fell to \$117.45. Beyond this point, the long call would have an advantage because its loss is capped at the price of the trade.

- In scenario 2, the stock rises \$30. Once again, the short put trade has a \$12.55 net advantage related to excess time premium realized as profit when the options expire. On the long call side, the \$6.85 of time premium that was paid for the initial trade is ultimately lost. The two trades would generate the same profit if the stock climbed to \$182.55. Beyond this point, the long call would have an advantage because the profit of the short put is capped at the price of the trade.
- Scenario 3 involves a modest \$15 price increase. Once again, the \$12.55 advantage is reflected in a larger profit for the short put trade. In this example, long stock only outperforms the short put trade if the stock rises above \$175.70.

These dynamics highlight the advantage of structuring long-term stock replacement trades with short deep in-the-money puts. DITM long calls had another disadvantage related to the implied volatility skew. The \$130 strike price options used in the example traded at 35% implied volatility whereas the \$170 strike was priced at 32%. This difference was responsible for the additional time value priced into the call side. We could have replicated this advantage in a shorter-term trade by using options that were closer to the trading price of the stock. This approach, however, reduces the amount of gain that can be realized by reducing the size of the credit.

Stock Replacement Summary

Most stock investors would be surprised to learn that they can achieve the goals of stock ownership using options, and that most option structures are both safer and more profitable. Simple stock ownership is always inferior and should be avoided unless options are not available. Many sophisticated investors avoid stocks that do not have listed options, and serious option traders almost never purchase a single share of stock.

Collars are clearly the safest approach. This trade structure caps both the maximum loss and gain at no additional cost. Investors who repeatedly structure short-term collars around a single stock tend to generate the largest profits because they have the opportunity to fine-tune their trades on a regular basis.

Covered calls are next on the list with sequential monthly sales providing a surprisingly strong gain that few stocks can match. A covered call trade structured with at-the-money options is mathematically identical to simply selling at the money puts. Investors who sell at the-money puts each month are likely to generate a much larger return than they could by owning the stock. Both approaches have unlimited downside risk.

Our review continued with synthetic stock positions composed of long calls and short puts. Synthetic stock conveys no particular advantage other than the reduced cost of the trade. This advantage is significant as it generally requires five times more money to purchase stock than to sell options.

Finally, our analysis of deep in-the-money long call or short put positions revealed a variety of choices that outperformed long stock in different ways under different circumstances. Long call trades are capped in terms of maximum loss while short put positions can generate profit from time decay. Knowledgeable investors vary their choices to accommodate changing market conditions.

These examples were meant to illustrate both the power of options and the limitations of traditional stock investing. The trades were chosen for their simplicity. In practice, most option traders structure more complex positions that take advantage of subtle differences between expiration dates and strike prices. Many of these strategies involve buying one month and selling another, buying one strike and selling another, or buying and selling different quantities at different strikes—structures commonly referred to as ratio trades.

By creating more complex structures, option traders are able to remove themselves from the more traditional game of betting on the direction of a stock or the market. Some of the trade structures presented above were designed around this theme. The approach of selling at-the-money puts is a perfect example. In principle, the trade is bullish because it profits most from a rise in the underlying stock price. Our goal, however, is to generate a large compounded return by selling new options each month. The examples presented above generate returns that are large enough to absorb virtually any downward move of the stock. They depend less on upward movement of the stock and more on the level of implied volatility priced into the options. Traders who pursue this and similar approaches spend the majority of their time analyzing the behavior of different stocks to identify candidates that they believe have overpriced options. Often the best candidates are stocks that have experienced large price declines. In such situations, uncertainty can cause high option prices to persist for extended periods of time after the stock has stabilized.

Evolving Strategies

On its surface, the previous discussion was about using options in place of stock. It was also designed around a more important theme, namely the evolution from trades that bet on direction to trades that profit from statistical advantages and price distortions. In the modern era, much more money is made by exploiting statistical advantages and subtle pricing inefficiencies than by predicting the direction of a financial instrument. Options, because of their statistical pricing basis, are one of the best vehicles for this type of trading.

Both institutional and private investors are becoming more sophisticated. The most powerful evidence of this trend is an explosion in the availability of exchange-traded derivatives that every investor has access to. Just a couple of years ago, private investors were discovering that they could hedge their stock bets by purchasing call options on the Chicago Board Options Exchange Volatility Index (VIX). These options have evolved from simple hedging vehicles to one of the most popular financial instruments. The open interest for VIX options expiring in August 2010 topped 1.5 million contracts. For comparison, U.S. Steel had only 75,000. Moreover, trading volatility has become so popular that ETFs have emerged to allow investors to buy and sell volatility in different time frames using predefined blends of futures contracts with different expirations. Volume in these funds is enormous with daily averages comfortably exceeding 20 million shares. These funds also have listed options. Typical retail investors, therefore, have exposure to VIX options, VIX futures, and options on VIX futures. Futures traders have even more choices.

Demand for volatility investment products, information, and new strategies has exploded. The CBOE has responded with a portfolio of products and technical information in the form of white papers and seminars. Following is a list of volatility indexes and related option products that were available at the time of this writing.[4]

CBOE Volatility Index (VIX)

CBOE Options on the CBOE Volatility Index

CBOE EuroCurrency Volatility Index (EVZ)

CBOE Gold Volatility Index (GVZ)

CBOE Crude Oil Volatility Index (OVX)

CBOE Binary Options on the CBOE Volatility Index (BVZ)

CBOE DJIA Volatility Index (VXD)

CBOE Nasdaq-100 Volatility Index (VXN)

CBOE Russell 2000 Volatility Index (RVX)

CBOE S&P 100 Volatility Index (VXO)

CBOE S&P 500 3-Month Volatility Index (VXV)

CBOE VIX Premium Strategy Index (VPD)

CBOE Capped VIX Premium Strategy Index (VPN)

CBOE S&P 500 VARB-X Strategy Benchmark (VTY)

CBOE S&P 500 Implied Correlation Index (ICJ, JCJ, KCJ)

CBOE Options on the iPath S&P 500 VIX Short-Term Futures Index ETN (VXX)

CBOE Options on the iPath S&P 500 VIX Mid-Term Futures Index ETN (VXZ)

Stock investors who are unaware of these indexes are blind to perhaps the most important set of indicators in the market. As we saw in Chapter 6, "The Importance of Volatility," the difference between actual volatility of the S&P 500 index and implied volatility of the options as represented by the VIX can be a significant measure of market uncertainty. Professional traders have focused on this difference for several years. Their interest stems from the observation that options implied volatility tends to be consistently larger than actual volatility of the market.

Activity in this area was strong enough to prompt the CBOE Futures Exchange (CFE) to introduce a product that allows investors to buy or sell the S&P 500's realized volatility over a period of three months. (CBOE S&P 500 Three-Month Variance Futures were introduced in June 2004.) More recently, the CBOE decided to extend this theme with a benchmark that tracks the performance of a hypothetical volatility arbitrage trading strategy designed to capitalize on the difference between implied volatility of S&P 500 index options and actual volatility of the index (CBOE S&P 500 VARB-XTM Strategy Benchmark).

Evolution of these trends has taken us from simple stock investing, to betting on volatility, to trading the difference between actual volatility and implied volatility of options on the broad market. Although the vast majority of investors will never trade this complex arbitrage, the benchmark, along with the VIX and other volatility indexes, provides a valuable set of indicators that everyone can learn to use.

It is also important to recognize that private investors are the primary audience for these complex trading products and indicators. Millions of retail customers now have trading platforms that can be used to buy and sell stocks, options, futures, options on futures, currencies, bonds, and a variety of other financial instruments. They can instantly display any of the indicators previously mentioned along with customized versions of their own design. Today's platforms also include programming languages that private investors can use to create their own technical indicators. In today's technical environment, a private individual with a reasonably priced computer and trading platform can discover subtle and complex relationships between the prices of financial instruments and build a new indicator that exploits the discovery. The trading can also be automated; most of today's platforms include a backtesting facility and tools for optimizing the parameters used to initiate and close trades. Many investors also use artificial intelligence software to spot complex and nearly invisible patterns that are unknown to the market. Discovering these patterns is a complex ongoing effort because each has a limited lifespan that depends on impossible-to-predict market dynamics.

Because the market is a zero sum game, individuals who limit themselves to using traditional off-the-shelf indicators will always lose money to sophisticated traders armed with more powerful tools. The days of buying and selling stocks when moving averages cross or an oscillator reaches one side of a channel are over. Moreover, investors who fool themselves into believing that they can exploit some combination of these indicators are making a huge mistake.

Superior trading tools are one part of the equation. But it is also important to recognize when your investment strategy conflicts with powerful forces that control the direction of the market. Most investors who shorted the housing market between 2004 and 2006 never realized that they were betting against the U.S. government. A broader view that included fiscal policy, currency exchange rates, the results of bond auctions, and the explosive growth of the credit default swap market might have steered them in the other direction. Politics also played a major role with debates in Congress signaling the government's desire to see a continued expansion of "the American dream of home ownership." In short, there was no attempt during this time frame to tighten the money supply or interfere with the lending process.

Sometimes the recognition of a powerful force can simplify the analysis. For example, between March 2009 and April 2010, Apple Computer climbed $185 (217%) dramatically outperforming the market. Along the way, many investors called the top and bet against the stock. In most cases, their reasons were related to financial metrics, increased competition, slowing of the economy, and other negative factors that they believed would cap the price of the stock. Half way through the rally, many investors and analysts were beginning to recognize that the stock price already comprehended several years of growth. The simple dynamic they were missing was Apple's position as one of the largest holdings at every major financial institution. Betting against Apple was tantamount to betting against Wall Street.

Investors who plan to bet against a stock should first make every attempt at understanding who lies on the other side of the trade. Expensive stocks that typically trade large blocks of shares tend to be owned by large institutions. If analysts are raising their price targets and brokerages are buying the stock for the portfolios of their largest investors, then a contrarian view is very dangerous. In Apple's case, the options market provided another important hint in the shape of the implied volatility skew. During most of the rally, out-of-the-money calls (higher strikes) were priced with increasingly higher implied volatility. Very distant strikes were considerably more expensive than at-the-money options. For many months, the options market continued pricing in $20–$40 increases while open interest and volume remained high in the most distant strikes. This information was immediately available to anyone who glanced at an option pricing screen that spanned a list of strike prices—the normal presentation format for most trading platforms. The skew finally flattened just before the rally ended.

Finally, unusual approaches are almost always risky. During the spectacular gold rally that took the price from $420 in 2005 to $1,000 in 2008, many investors lost money betting on small gold companies, also known as "the minors." They carefully researched each company, pouring through the numbers and business information. In most cases, their investment decisions were based on sound financial reasoning and an accurate view of the market. Unfortunately, they missed one important dynamic—the behavior of large institutional investors who often bought stock in the major players and shorted the minors as a hedge. Each time the market fell, these investors bought more large company stocks; rallies created new opportunities to short the smaller companies at more favorable prices. Their buying and selling behavior had the effect of stabilizing the majors during corrections and depressing the minors when the market was rising. Once again, the problem was betting against a powerful force.

Endnotes

1. If options were not identically priced, opportunities would exist for risk-free arbitrage trades. The execution of these trades would immediately erase the difference. Tiny differences such as the $0.10 between the put and call pair in the first entry are too small to be exploited by retail customers who pay trading fees and commissions.

2. A short call is also covered when the account is long another call on the same security with the same or lower strike and the same or later expiration.
3. The average amount of time premium in each weekly option is calculated across the range from $5 out-of-the-money to $5 in-the-money. For in-the-money options, the distance to the strike is subtracted from the option price to determine the amount of time premium in the option contracts. This approach is more precise than simply using the value of at-the-money options because the stock can potentially trade anywhere in the range on Thursday morning when each new weekly series becomes available.
4. http://www.cboe.com/micro/IndexSites.aspx.

Appendix A

Options Primer

Some of the discussions in this book mention put and call options. In every case, the complexity has been kept to a minimum and lengthy mathematical discussions of option pricing theory have been avoided. However, some terminology and basic principles are important for all investors to understand. This appendix is designed to address those needs with basic definitions and information about the dynamics that affect option pricing.

Most introductory option trading books follow a different approach. They devote the bulk of their discussion to specific trade structures. Many of the structures they describe are complex in the sense that they include both puts and calls with different expirations spanning multiple strike prices. Attempting to structure such trades without a firm grasp of the underlying pricing dynamics is dangerous. This assertion applies to even the simplest option trade—the purchase of a put or call.

Consider, for example, the case where someone who is new to options decides to purchase calls as a bullish bet on a stock. Those calls have a price that is determined by the time remaining before expiration, the strike price of the option, and both the price and underlying volatility of the stock. Many investors make the mistake of ignoring these factors. They rely on their opinion about the performance of a stock to choose a strike price and expiration month for the option. This decision ignores factors like time decay and volatility. Moreover, they might not realize that volatility affects the price of a call option, and that volatility tends to decline in a rising market. Investors often lose money trading options even after making the right decision about the direction of the underlying stock.

Simply stated, you cannot effectively trade a financial instrument without understanding the factors that affect its price. This appendix is designed to address the problem for equity and index options by focusing on basic pricing theory. We will also review the elements that define the behavior of an option contract over time as value of the underlying security varies. These elements, also known as "the Greeks," provide key metrics that can be used to predict how an option's price will be affected by the market and the behavior of the underlying security.

Black-Scholes Pricing Model

In 1973, a landmark paper published by Fischer Black and Myron Scholes in the *Journal of Political Economy* revolutionized the world of derivatives pricing with a rigorous and extensible mathematical framework. The paper proposed a new model that quantified the influence and interaction of both time and uncertainty. The model, which was later extended in several important directions by Robert Merton, eventually became the foundation for modern option pricing across all markets—equities, indexes, and futures. Merton's extensions addressed options with dividends, nonconstant interest rate environments, and more general structures for pricing other contingent contracts. Myron Scholes and Robert Merton were ultimately awarded the 1997 Nobel Prize in Economic Sciences for their combined contributions to "A New Method to Determine the Value of Derivatives." (Fischer Black died in 1995.)

Although many other pricing models have evolved over the years, Black-Scholes remains the gold standard. Every modern trading platform can calculate option prices using the Black-Scholes model. However, like any model, Black-Scholes and its descendents have flaws. Most criticism centers around the assumption that price changes are random and closely follow the normal distribution.

The Black-Scholes model was also designed around European-style options, which can only be exercised at the end of the contract time frame. The calculations can be adjusted to account for American-style options, which are always exercisable. However, because early exercise of an in-the-money option involves throwing away the remaining time premium, it rarely occurs. Today's option pricing models contain many other inefficiencies as well—most are unavoidable. These inefficiencies sometimes yield price distortions that can be profitably traded.

Calls and Puts

Call options are contracts that entitle the buyer to purchase stock at a predetermined price, also known as the strike price. Put options entitle the buyer to sell stock at the strike price. The fair value of an option, call or put, can be determined using a mathematical model that takes into account the price and volatility of the underlying security, time until expiration of the contract, and the risk-free interest rate that the money could otherwise earn. Actual trading prices of options can differ considerably from theoretical predictions, especially when the market anticipates a large move of the stock. These distortions often precede earnings announcements and other significant events. Under these circumstances, option pricing dynamics can seem foreign to stock investors because option prices can rise and fall without any change in the underlying stock price.

The difference between implied volatility of an option contract and historical volatility of a stock often becomes a point of confusion. Historical volatility is calculated using the price change history of the underlying security. This value along with the other key parameters—stock price, strike price of the option, time remaining before contract expiration, and risk free interest—can be entered into one of the mathematical models to determine a fair option price. Conversely, the actual trading price of an option can be used to calculate its implied volatility.

In the simplest terms, an investor who pays $10 for a $100 call option expects the stock to trade above $110 at expiration. Conversely, the same investor would pay $10 for a $100 put if he expected the stock to fall below $90 by expiration. On the final day, when the time value has all run out, an in-the-money option will trade for a value very close to its in-the-money amount. At this point, in-the-money options take on the value of the underlying stock. Because each contract represents 100 shares of stock, an investor who owns 10 contracts of a $10 in-the-money option would have a position equivalent to 1,000 shares of stock.

Put options are somewhat equivalent to short shares. An investor holding 10 put contracts on a stock trading $10 below the strike price would have a position that is equivalent to being short 1,000 shares of the underlying stock.

Some option traders use these dynamics to structure stock-equivalent option positions at reduced prices. The advantage becomes clear with expensive stocks. Consider, for example, the difference between the cost of 100 shares of a $200 stock and the cost of 1 call trading $50 in-the-money ($150 strike price for a $200 stock). Purchasing the stock would cost $20,000 while the deep in-the-money options would cost approximately $5,000. Deep in the-money calls were chosen for this example because they typically have almost no time premium regardless of the number of days remaining before expiration.

Instead of buying deep in-the-money calls, a bullish option trader might choose to sell puts that are just as far in-the-money for $50. This position, because it has no long option to cap its potential loss, is considered "naked." Naked calls can lose an unlimited amount of money because, theoretically, there is no limit to the amount a stock can rise. Naked puts have a loss limit because the stock cannot fall below zero. Certain types of accounts such as IRAs are restricted in the sense that they cannot hold naked call positions. However, these accounts can sell puts if they have enough money to cover purchasing the underlying stock. The position would be referred to as "cash covered." In nonrestricted accounts, naked call positions must be "collateralized" with a certain amount of cash. Collateral requirements can be precisely calculated. Readers who are interested in learning more about collateral requirements for different kinds of structured positions are encouraged to visit the Chicago Board Options Exchange website at www.CBOE.com.

Implied Versus Historical Volatility

Trading platforms always display the actual trading price along with a calculated value for implied volatility. Experienced option traders constantly compare these values to their own estimates that are based on the stock's price change behavior in a number of different time frames and situations. Estimating the fair value of an option is sometimes more art than science. It is also one of the most valuable investing skills a trader can have. Consider the following example:

On July 22, 2010, after the market closed, Amazon reported disappointing earnings with the stock trading just above $120. The next morning the stock opened more than $14 lower at $106. Before the announcement, $110 puts were priced around $1.35 (35% implied volatility). The implied volatility was about 5% higher than it would have been without an approaching earnings announcement. Unfortunately, the options market completely underestimated the risk because when the market opened with the stock trading at $106, the $110 puts skyrocketed to more than $6.00. The correct implied volatility for these options on the previous day would have been 77%. At that level, sellers would have been fairly compensated for risk because the $110 puts would have traded for $6.00—the price they ultimately reached after the announcement.

Amazon missed its earnings forecast while posting exceptional revenue growth. After the announcement and the sharp correction, the stock rebounded, ultimately returning to its original pre-announcement price. Insightful traders who followed both the industry and the company understood the complexity of the situation. Amazon was expanding into new markets and battling fierce competitors like Apple and Google. Following their growth, expenses, expansion, and product development roadmaps were essentially impossible. The stock was also trading with a very high PE ratio—nearly 50. Finally, the situation was further complicated by a variety of accounting changes that affected the way revenue was recognized and fulfillment expenses were reported. In short, no rational trader would price this kind of a situation at 35% implied volatility.

Amazon's earnings story highlights the most important difference between options and stock—options are priced according to risk; stocks are not. Option prices have a large number of moving parts that must all be understood in addition to the variables that also impact the underlying stock price.

One of the most important and frequently misunderstood concepts about options is their value as a separate financial instrument. Every option, call or put, has a value and can be traded. Very few options are ever exercised by public customers because exercising an option means throwing away its residual value in terms of remaining time premium. Suppose, for example, that an investor owns a call with a strike price of $100 and 3 months remaining before expiration on a stock that has risen to $104. In option trading terms, the call is $4 "in-the-money." The option, however, will have a value somewhat higher than $4. This additional value is a product of remaining time and volatility priced into the contracts. In most cases the difference is substantial. A $100 call with 90 days remaining before expiration, priced with 35% implied volatility, on a $104 stock, would be worth $9.27—considerably more than the amount the stock is in-the-money. Increasing the volatility to 40% raises the price to $10.25. An investor who exercises this option would be throwing away $6.25 of "time premium." On expiration day, after all time premium has run out, the very last trade of any option contract is typically into the hands of a broker who can exercise the contracts without paying transaction costs.

Calls and puts are always priced with the same implied volatility at a given strike price. This relationship, known as put-call parity, prevents the execution of a risk-free arbitrage. If, for example, the put side were to be priced out of proportion to the call, then a savvy investor would sell the put and buy the call while simultaneously selling the stock and buying a riskless zero-coupon bond maturing in the expiration time frame of the option. The position would be unwound at the time of options expiration for a guaranteed profit. Although parity disruptions occasionally appear, public customers who buy at the asking price and sell at the bidding price are unable to take advantage of the opportunity because it is normally accompanied by uncharacteristically wide bid-ask spreads.

Calls are always slightly more expensive than puts. The reason is simple: A $10 stock that experiences two 50% price declines will trade for $2.50. However, if the same stock experiences two 50% increases, it will trade for $22.50. The decrease ($7.50) is much smaller than the increase ($12.50). These dynamics make sense because a stock can never trade for less than $0.00.

Historical volatility, the basis for option pricing, is based on the log of the price change. It assumes that the logs of the price changes fit the normal distribution. This distribution, which takes the form of a bell curve, is the basis for all option pricing. If we assumed that actual price changes were normally distributed instead of the logs of the price changes, then negative prices would be possible and option pricing theory would fail.

Adoption of the normal distribution for option pricing has far-reaching implications. Underlying the mathematics of a random distribution is the assumption that the market is efficient and the evolution of prices cannot be predicted. This assertion and a descriptive model that includes different forms of efficiency were popularized by Burton Malkiel in a 1973 book entitled *A Random Walk Down Wall Street*. Since that time, there have been many debates between proponents of the theory and investors/theorists who believe that they can identify chart patterns with predictive power. However, for a chart pattern to have predictive power, it must also be persistent in the sense that the market cannot learn the pattern and eliminate it. Such patterns run counter to the random walk because they represent a market inefficiency. The random walk concept is built on an important set of assertions known as the efficient market hypothesis (EMH). EMH predicts that such inefficiencies cannot persist. It was first proposed by Eugene Fama in his Ph.D. thesis at the University of Chicago Graduate School of Business in the early 1960s.

Figure A.1 depicts the lognormal distribution in terms of standard deviations and probability. The chart marks major intervals of 1, 2, and 3 standard deviations. Looking at the curve, for example, we can determine that 34% of all price changes will fall between 0 and –1 standard deviation. The probability, therefore, of a 1 standard deviation change in either direction is 68%. Modern spreadsheets such as Excel have a normal distribution function that can give precise probabilities for any size change.

Option traders always think in standard deviations and probabilities. The conversion from implied or historical volatility to standard deviations is relatively straightforward; volatility is equal to the value of a 1-year, 1 standard deviation price change of the underlying stock. For a $100 stock with 30% historical volatility, this value would equal $30. Using the normal distribution we would conclude that the stock has a 68% probability of ending the year between $70 and $130. This value is derived from Figure A.1 by multiplying the probability of the price change falling between 0 and –1 standard deviation. Extending our analysis to 2 standard deviations yields a 95% chance that the stock will end up between $40 and $160. The calculation yields a value of more than 99% for a 3 standard deviation change (49.87% x 2).

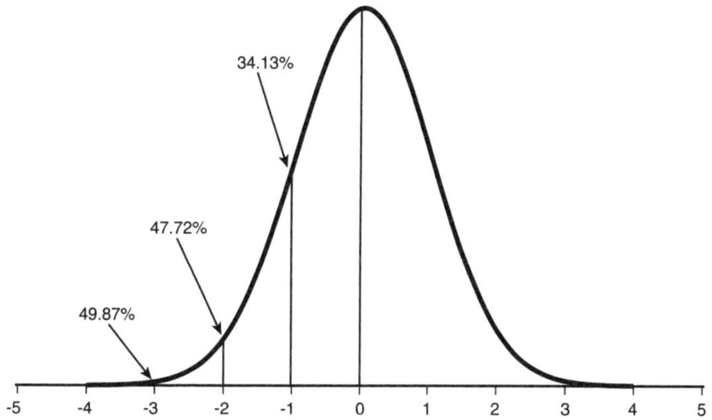

FIGURE A.1 *Normal distribution curve with standard deviations displayed on the x-axis. Probabilities are marked for downward price changes of 1, 2, and 3 standard deviations.*

Because volatility is proportional to the square root of time, we can derive the value for a shorter time frame by dividing the annual value by the square root of the number of shorter time frames contained in 1 year. To calculate monthly volatility we would divide annual volatility by the square root of 12; weekly volatility would be equal to annual volatility divided by the square root of 52. Assuming 252 trading days per year, the value of a daily 1 standard deviation price change for a $100 stock with 30% implied volatility would be

$100 x 0.30 / Sqrt(252) = $1.89. The value of a 1-month, 1 standard deviation change would be given by $100 x 0.30 / Sqrt(12) = $8.66.[1]

Traditional option pricing theory stumbles here because it predicts that a 3 standard deviation change will occur less than once each year. We would, therefore, expect a $100 stock with 30% implied volatility to experience a $5.67 price change less often than once in an entire trading year. Larger changes in the range of 4 or 5 standard deviations should never occur. But in real life, such changes occur much more frequently than the model predicts. These outlying changes alter the shape of the distribution so that the tails at the extreme edges never really touch the x-axis. Option traders refer to these distortions in the distribution as "fat tails."

Skewed Volatility—The Volatility "Smile"

The market has responded to this tendency for standard pricing models to fail at the extremes by adding risk in the form of implied volatility to out-of-the-money options. This correction, commonly referred to as a volatility skew or "smile," has a distinctive shape that can be visualized in a plot of implied volatility as a function of strike price.

The volatility smile became much more pronounced after the stock market crash of October 1987 when out-of-the-money puts climbed steeply in value. Since then, implied volatility profiles for equity and index options have taken on a distinctly negative skew—that is, volatility tends to rise as the strike price decreases. This effect causes out-of-the-money puts to be relatively more expensive than Black-Scholes theory predicts. Additionally, since put-call parity dictates that the relationship between strike price and implied volatility is the same for both types of contracts, in-the-money calls are also more expensive.

The term "smile" is sometimes misleading when out-of-the-money puts are more expensive than out-of-the-money calls. For most stocks the smile flattens just beyond the current trading price of the stock. However, options on stocks that exhibit a large number of upward price change surprises are often priced with a symmetrical smile where out-of-the-money prices are inflated for both puts and calls. The form of the smile is different for other financial instruments. Currency options, for example, are priced with a symmetrical volatility increase centered at-the-money. Volatility increases whether an option moves in or out of the money. Commodity options also tend to be priced with a symmetrical smile. The chance of a large upward price spike of gold, for example, is considered at least as likely as the chance of a downward spike.

The volatility smile represents an important distortion of the Black-Scholes pricing model. Out-of-the-money calls tend to be heavily discounted for most stocks because the chance of a crash up is much smaller than the chance of a crash down. From a trading perspective, this distortion can be interpreted to mean that implied volatility will fall if the stock (or the market) rises. Conversely, the high values placed on low strike prices are an indication that volatility can be expected to rise when the market falls. This behavior is evident in most stocks, equity indexes, and the closely followed CBOE Volatility Index (VIX). The form of the smile is different for other financial instruments.

Term Structure

It is important to distinguish between smile and term structure, which measures the effect of time on implied volatility. Term structure can be visualized in a plot of implied volatility for at-the-money options versus expiration month. Its behavior tends to compress the shape of the smile curve as the maturity date increases. If we create a family of volatility smile curves, one curve per month, we will find that the shape of the curve becomes less pronounced as time advances. Experienced traders sometimes use this information to create a table containing the correct implied volatility for each expiration date and strike price. The ultimate goal is to construct complex three-dimensional maps that relate implied volatility to calendar information and price of the underlying security. These maps, or volatility surfaces as they are commonly known, are an important tool for determining the fair value of an option. Over time, the maps accumulate and form a library of surfaces that can be used to analyze specific market conditions. For example, a three-dimensional map can be constructed with strike prices on the x-axis, term to expiration on the y-axis, and implied volatility on the z-axis (vertical axis). The map would be specific to a particular date and set of market conditions. At a later date when the market and, more important the individual security, displayed similar characteristics, the map could be retrieved for comparison to actual trading prices. These maps often reveal repeating oscillations that can be used to predict rising and falling implied volatility.

The Greeks

Various characteristics of an option position can be described using parameters derived from the Black-Scholes formulas. Each parameter is an important component in the overall risk picture. As a group they relate information about the effects of price, volatility, and interest rate changes, in addition to time decay. Risk assessment of an option position commonly takes the form of descriptions that utilize the Greeks. For example, a trader might describe an option position as being "delta short 100 shares of stock." Such a position, because of its delta and size, will respond to initial price changes in the underlying as if it were 100 shares of stock. Each of the Greeks is briefly described in Table A.1.

TABLE A.1 *Brief Description of the Greeks*

Greek	Description
Delta	Effect of a $1 increase in the underlying
Gamma	Effect of a $1 increase in the Delta
Vega	Effect of a 1% increase in volatility
Theta	Rate of time decay (usually expressed in dollars per day)
Rho	Effect of a 1% increase in interest rate

Although each of the Greeks is important, some figure more prominently in most discussions. Rho, for instance, tends to become significant only if interest rates are very high (for example, the early 1980s when rho hovered near 20%), or if substantial interest rate changes are expected during the life of the options being traded. Conversely, delta and theta are important components of virtually every option position. Gamma, which describes the rate of change of delta, is very important for risk management and hedging. We will discuss each of these parameters in the sections that follow.

Delta

Delta represents the amount that the option price will change if the underlying moves $1. Suppose, for example, an investor wishes to purchase 10 contracts of $100 strike price calls under the following conditions:

Current date = 2010/12/08 at 9:30 A.M.

Expiration date = 2010/12/18 at 11:59:00 P.M.

Days left = 10.60

Underlying trading at $98.50

Underlying volatility = 40%

Risk free interest = 0.15%

The Black-Scholes formula sets the delta of the calls at 0.43 and the price at $2.02. Since 1 contract represents 100 shares, the cost of the trade will be $2.02 x 10 contracts x 100 shares per contract = $2020. An instantaneous $1.00 upward move of the stock will adjust the position value by $0.43 to $2.45. The trade would now be worth $2,450. An investor who sold 10 contracts would experience a $430 loss. The situation is actually more complex since the delta will change with the stock price. The precise Black-Scholes calculation actually reveals that the option price will move a slightly larger

$0.45. After the move, the new delta will be 0.49. Another $1 increase will raise the delta to 0.54.

An investor taking a short position on 10 contracts of these calls could fully hedge his initial position by purchasing 43% of the number of shares represented in the option contracts (that is, .43 x 1,000 shares = 430 shares). However, as we have just seen, each move of the stock will cause the delta to change. Maintaining a perfect hedge, therefore, can become a challenge. A large upward move of the stock will raise the delta to 1.00, and a perfect hedge will require a long position of 1,000 shares. It is precisely for this reason that many investors track the gamma of a position. Many short sellers actually hedge with options so that both the hedge and the short position experience similar changes in delta. We will return to a discussion of hedging and gamma in the next section.

Delta is also affected by time. In the previous example, if the stock were to stay at $98.50 until expiration, both the delta and the value of the option would fall. At expiration the option would be worthless because it is below the strike price. The relationship between time and delta is not linear—the decay accelerates as the contract nears expiration. Figure A.2 depicts the relationship between time and delta for the $100 strike price option previously specified.

Each data point in Figure A.2 was calculated at 9:30 in the morning (the market open). Such precision is unnecessary when evaluating option positions that have a significant amount of time left until expiration. However, in the final few days, and especially on the last day, precise calculations can be very important. Many of today's sophisticated pricing programs use the number of seconds until expiration for their calculations. Monthly equity and index options expire at 11:59 P.M. on the Saturday following the third Friday of each month. During the final few days before expiration, a significant amount of time decay occurs each evening during the 17.5 hours that the market is closed. The effect can be very significant for options on indexes or expensive stocks where a significant amount of time value remains until the last few hours. The effect is especially significant during the final weekend before expiration when at-the-money options lose nearly 30% of their remaining value. This distortion frequently causes prices to collapse near the close on Friday as buyers factor in the value that will be lost before the market opens on Monday.

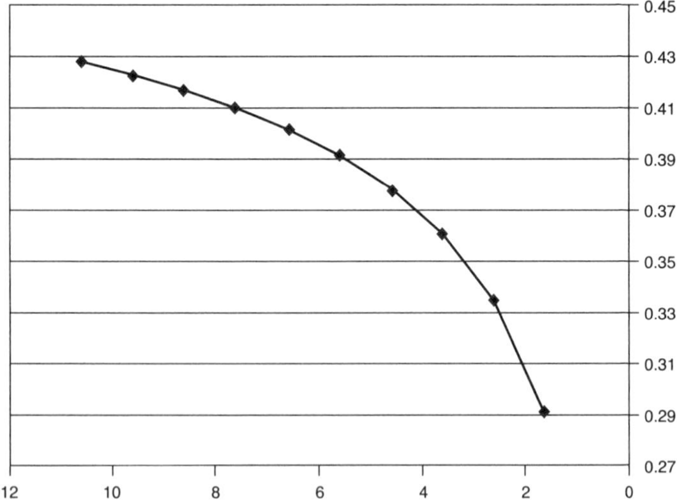

FIGURE A.2 *The relationship between time decay and delta. Days remaining before expiration are depicted on the x-axis and delta on the y-axis for a $100 strike price call priced with 40% implied volatility on a stock trading at $98.50.*

As one would expect, put deltas move opposite call deltas—they rise when a stock falls and fall when a stock rises. Put and call deltas, however, are not symmetrical. This subtlety, which is related to the lognormal distribution, is very important to understand Suppose, for example, that we wanted to find the delta-neutral stock price for option contracts with a strike price of $130, 192 days remaining until expiration, priced with 30% volatility. According to the Black-Scholes formulas, put and call deltas would each be 0.50 if the stock were trading at $123.62—more than $6 below the strike price. Setting the stock price at $130 would generate a call delta of 0.59 and a put delta of 0.41. In both cases the option prices are different. The delta-neutral case yields a call price of $9.41 and a put price of $12.41 while the $130 stock price case yields $12.90 and $9.62, respectively. This asymmetry of price and delta is related to the lognormal distribution.

Gamma

Gamma is a measure of the rate of change of delta with respect to the price of the underlying. Most option pricing programs determine gamma by calculating delta, incrementing the stock price $1.00, and repeating the calculation. Subtracting the first delta from the second yields gamma. Put and call gammas are always equal both in magnitude and sign.

Option traders who ignore the effect of gamma run the risk of underestimating risk. In the 1987 stock market drawdown, many option traders lost huge amounts of money because they were short large amounts of gamma. Traders who were short both puts and calls initially had insignificant losses if put and call deltas were similar. However, as downward price movements continued, call deltas fell quickly and put deltas rose to 1. A short position composed of 10 puts and 10 calls rapidly became equivalent to a position that was short 1,000 shares of stock. A careful analysis of gamma would have caused many of these traders to tighten their stop orders in anticipation of a potentially catastrophic rise in gamma. Unfortunately, many option traders take the more simplistic view that a short option position is safe as long as the option remains out-of-the-money. However, a more careful risk assessment that takes into account the position gamma often reveals that the value of the contract can double or triple without breaching the strike price. Conversely, the most successful hedges are those that are long large amounts of gamma. Such positions benefit from large underlying price changes that raise the position delta. The goal is to establish a relatively inexpensive position that has the potential to grow rapidly and offset losses. An example would be the purchase of a large number of inexpensive far-out-of-the-money puts that can be expected to achieve a high delta in the event of a market collapse.

Figure A.3 compares the effect of time on delta and gamma. The risks associated with a short position rise rapidly in the final few days preceding expiration as the delta falls and the gamma rises. The implications are wide ranging for a variety of complex positions that involve options expiring in different months. For example, a popular trade involves purchasing long dated options and selling each month's options to pay for the time decay. The risk of such a position increases dramatically as expiration approaches because a large move of the underlying can rapidly raise the delta of the short contracts while having very small offsetting effects on the long side of the trade. Positions that span different strike prices and months with long and short components are, therefore, very sensitive to the timing of moves of the underlying stock or index. Complex multipart positions can only be managed by traders who understand the effects of time on both delta and gamma.

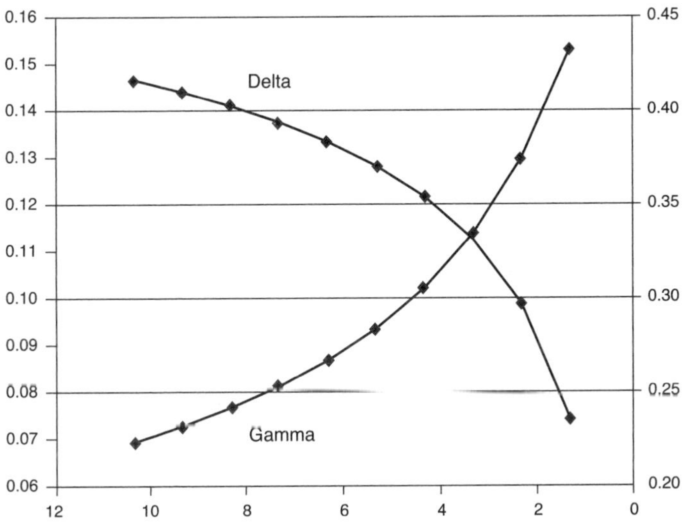

FIGURE A.3 *Comparison of the effect of time on delta and gamma. Days remaining before expiration are depicted on the x-axis, gamma on the left y-axis, and delta on the right y-axis. The calculations are for a $100 strike price call on a stock with 34% implied volatility trading at $98.50.*

Vega

Vega measures the effect of changing volatility on the price of an option. There actually is no letter in the Greek alphabet called "vega," so some analysts use the symbol tau instead. Vega measures the change in option price for a 1% change in volatility. A vega of 0.25 indicates that the option price will increase $0.25 when implied volatility rises 1%. As with the other Greeks, a simple calculation can be performed by solving the Black-Scholes formula at two different volatilities and subtracting the smaller result from the larger. Vega, like gamma, is the same for puts and calls.

Vega is affected both by time and price of the underlying. Far-out-of-the-money and deep in-the-money options are both characterized by very small vega—neither is very sensitive to changes in volatility. Similarly, at-the-money options become much less sensitive to changes in volatility as expiration approaches, while the same strike price option with several months remaining will be very sensitive to volatility changes in the underlying. Tracking vega is essential when trading positions that are based on anticipated changes in volatility.

Theta

Theta describes time decay of an option contract. Many books have stated that theta is an enemy of an option holder and a friend of an option seller. This view represents a dangerous oversimplification. While theta is certainly destructive to long positions, it also represents risk exposure to short positions.

Theta is written as a negative number. An option contract with a theta of –0.10 loses 10 cents per day of time value. Furthermore, an option contract that has 30 days remaining before expiration and trades for $3.00 must necessarily exhibit a theta of –.10 or 10 cents per day. Theta, therefore, is dramatically affected by the price of the underlying. As one might expect, deep in or out-of-the-money options have very little theta. This effect becomes exaggerated as expiration draws near. As before, the most efficient method for determining theta involves calculating the option price, advancing the time by 1 day, repeating the calculation, and subtracting the second result from the first.

Rho

Rho relates the change of an option's value to changing interest rates. Call rho is positive and put rho is negative. As one might expect, deep out-of-the-money options are relatively insensitive to interest rate changes while deep in-the-money options are very sensitive. Likewise, long-term options have a larger rho than short-term options. Most discussions neglect the effects of interest rate changes because they tend to be relatively small and infrequent. However, during economic cycles characterized by persistently climbing or falling interest rates, the effect on long-term options can be pronounced.

Summary

Option traders generally fall into two distinct categories. The first includes stock investors who use options to complement existing strategies; the second is populated with technical traders who rarely employ stocks as primary investment vehicles. The two groups differ dramatically with regard to their investment goals and approaches.

Stock investors who also trade options tend to have bullish or bearish opinions. They often rely on fundamental or technical analysis to make trading decisions and choose stocks for long or short positions. For these investors, options are often used as a hedge against existing stock positions. They can also be used as a proxy to create lower cost trades that have more leverage.

Technical option traders tend to structure direction-neutral positions that profit across a wide range of conditions. They manage their trades by calculating risk in terms of position delta and gamma. These investors sometimes use stocks to make fine adjustments to complex option positions. Their approach to investing is dramatically different because it doesn't involve "stock picking."

Investors who occasionally complement stock trades with options often make the mistake of ignoring the complex dynamics of option pricing. This approach always fails because it involves trading a financial instrument without understanding exactly how it will respond to varying market conditions. Because option prices are influenced by a variety of factors such as time remaining before expiration and volatility, an option contract can lose value even if the stock moves in the expected direction. Moreover, option prices can rise or fall without any change in the price of the underlying security.

This appendix is designed to address these issues by providing an overview of the key elements that determine how an option contract responds to changes in the price of the underlying security. Interested investors are encouraged to pursue more detailed studies of option pricing theory and to use this appendix as a guide.

Endnotes

1. There is some disagreement about the adjustment factor for daily volatility because a calendar year contains approximately 252 trading days. Using this number we would divide by 15.87 to obtain daily volatility, which is also equal to the value of a close-to-close 1 standard deviation price change.

INDEX

G

H

I

T

U–V

W–Z